D0988964

The Creative Journal for Parents

Other Works by Dr. Lucia Capacchione

BOOKS

THE CREATIVE JOURNAL:
THE ART OF FINDING YOURSELF

THE CREATIVE JOURNAL FOR CHILDREN:
A GUIDE FOR PARENTS, TEACHERS, AND COUNSELORS

THE CREATIVE JOURNAL FOR TEENS

LIGHTEN UP YOUR BODY, LIGHTEN UP YOUR LIFE
(with Elizabeth Johnson and James Strohecker)

THE PICTURE OF HEALTH:
HEALING YOUR LIFE WITH ART

THE POWER OF YOUR OTHER HAND

PUTTING YOUR TALENT TO WORK
(with Peggy Van Pelt)

RECOVERY OF YOUR INNER CHILD

VISIONING: TEN STEPS TO DESIGNING THE
LIFE OF YOUR DREAMS

THE WELL-BEING JOURNAL: DRAWING ON YOUR INNER
POWER TO HEAL YOURSELF

AUDIOTAPES

THE PICTURE OF HEALTH (meditation and journal exercises)

THE WISDOM OF YOUR OTHER HAND (set of five tapes)

The Creative Journal for Parents

A GUIDE TO UNLOCKING YOUR NATURAL PARENTING WISDOM

Lucia Capacchione

SHAMBHALA
Boston & London
2000

SHAMBHALA PUBLICATIONS, INC.
Horticultural Hall
300 Massachusetts Avenue
Boston, Massachusetts 02115
www.shambhala.com

For information about Lucia Capacchione's lectures,
workshops, and professional training, contact:
Lucia Capacchione
P.O. Box 1355
Cambria, CA 93428
(805) 546-1424
Or visit the Web site at *www.luciac.com*.

© *2000 by Lucia Capacchione*
All rights reserved.
No part of this book may be reproduced
in any form or by any means,
electronic or mechanical, including photocopying, recording,
or by any information storage and retrieval system,
without permission in writing from the publisher.

9 8 7 6 5 4 3 2 1

First Edition

Printed in the United States of America
⊗ *This edition is printed on acid-free paper that meets*
the American National Standards Institute Z39.48 Standard.
Distributed in the United States by Random House, Inc.,
and in Canada by Random House of Canada Ltd.

T O

my grandparents and parents
(especially my mother, Connie Capacchione),
my children, Celia and Aleta,
and my grandchildren.
It was through being parented
and through parenting
that I have learned
the greatest lessons life has to teach.

CONTENTS

The Creative Journal for Parents

I N T R O D U C T I O N

Readers of my earlier books think of me as an art therapist, originator of the Creative Journal Method and Inner Family work. What most people *don't* know is that I entered the field of art therapy through the door of early childhood education and parent education. My concern with child development and parenting began for a very personal reason: I became pregnant. It was my passion for finding out everything I could about being a mother myself that led me into the field professionally.

I was twenty-three and working as a staff designer for Charles Eames, famous for his chairs, films, and exhibits. Recently married and planning a family, I wanted some experience with children, so I offered to lead Saturday children's art workshops at an inner-city parochial school. I waited for an answer from the school. On New Year's Day of 1961, the principal called and offered me a full-time job as fourth grade teacher of forty-six children. I had a degree in art with no training or experience in education, and I already had a prestigious job in the nation's top design office at a higher salary. It was an extremely unlikely career move. Yet I said yes. Afterward I was more shocked than anyone else that I had accepted the position.

Later I learned why the previous teacher had resigned: she'd had a "nervous breakdown" over the Christmas holidays. The principal was desperate, which was why my inexperience and lack of training had been so unimportant. Lucky for me, because it turned out to be the opportunity of a lifetime. I knew nothing about teaching. After bungling my way through for a few weeks, I resorted to the familiar and began experimenting. I taught basic skills and school subjects through *art* (which was something I did know about). Within a few weeks, classroom discipline problems were greatly reduced. Grades went up, and it was obvious that learning had become fun for my students. Teaching became fun, too. It didn't hurt that my last project at the Eames office was a 3-D math exhibit along with films for IBM that were targeted for children as young as eight.

That one semester of teaching elementary school was an experience I will never forget. I am eternally grateful to those forty-six children for teaching me everything I know about education and about how kids learn. The hand of God was clearly shaping these events. I simply heard the call.

Thus began my second career. As soon as it started, it appeared to be over. By the end of the school year, I was six months pregnant. We moved to a bigger place and prepared for the birth of our daughter, Celia. In my book *The Picture of Health: Healing Your Life with Art,* I described what happened next:

> We were living in a semirural area far from the city, friends and familiar places. I felt very isolated while recovering from the difficult delivery of our first child. I can remember being overwhelmed by postpartum depression as I stood at the clothesline in the field behind our country cottage. The diapers hanging on the line seemed to stretch out into infinity. My college education and exciting career in design had never prepared me for this. Talk about "the blues"! I was asking myself, "What's wrong with this picture?"
>
> . . . I turned inward and realized that I still had the power to create. It had always pulled me out of difficult times before, and it would pull me out again. So during the baby's naps, I started doing artwork. At the kitchen table, next to piles of clean diapers and rows of baby bottles, I

designed and printed greeting cards. In no time my creative juices were flowing and the depression lifted. The cards were accepted by shops and mail order companies, and I launched a part-time career as a freelance artist. Motherhood became a great adventure instead of an overwhelming burden, and a year later we had our second child, Aleta.

While delivering greeting cards to a retail shop one day, I struck up a conversation with the owner, Steve. I was carrying Celia in my arms, and he remarked on how beautiful she was. "And look at those eyes. She looks so bright," Steve exclaimed. "Of course, you're going to send her to a Montessori school." While working on the math exhibit during my design office days, I had been told about Maria Montessori, who had created some incredible educational materials around the turn of the century. Her books hadn't been published in the United States yet, so I'd never been able to find information about her method. Steve turned to the shelf behind him, reached over to a section labeled "Montessori," and grabbed a book. "Here, you'll need this," he said, handing me a copy of *The Absorbent Mind.* I opened it and saw that it had been published in Madras, India, by the Theosophical Press. The pages were thin and smelled faintly of incense. Steve told me about Dr. Montessori's philosophy and described her open classroom filled with exquisitely designed self-teaching materials. He rhapsodized about her discovery: children have within them a natural desire to learn and an inner impulse that leads them to what they need at any given time.

It all seemed rather exotic and mysterious, but I knew I had been given a gift that I would treasure for the rest of my life. Later I pored over that first Montessori book, and then I got two more. I couldn't get enough information about how children learn and was experiencing my own "absorbent mind" firsthand. Of course, my home was the perfect laboratory for experimenting with Montessori's theories. I found myself observing my children's every move. I charted the dates and new skills they were acquiring on graph paper calendars: "Discovers her own hand and seems to understand that she can control it. . . . Recognizes herself in the mirror and laughs. . . . Says first word: *cookie*. . . . Recognizes a photo of herself and says her own name. . . . Draws a circle with a pencil."

I also set up their room like a mini-Montessori school, with shelves of stimulating educational materials, building toys, and books. A corner of the kitchen had an easel and art supplies for them to use whenever they wished. Our home was a "prepared environment" for learning and creative expression. My husband and I even developed some geodesic construction toys for the girls, which were later put on the market.

When our second daughter, Aleta, was still an infant, I began seriously researching Montessori preschools, which were just beginning to appear in California. The year was 1963. I quickly found that Montessori education was in great demand. We got the girls on the waiting list of our local school long before they were old enough to attend. If we hadn't, they might not have been admitted when the time came. It was the era of Sputnik, the Cold War was raging, and America was engaged in an intense "space race" with the Soviet Union. Affluent, educated parents were obsessed with getting their preschoolers into Harvard (or some such prestigious school) someday. This atmosphere was fertile ground for the Montessori schools that sprang up throughout the United States in the next few years. I feel certain that Montessori herself would have been horrified at the extreme pressure some of these affluent parents were placing on their so-called privileged children. After all, she had invented the "open classroom," where the operating principle was free choice and individually determined purposeful activity. Teachers were supposed to facilitate learning, not force-feed it.

Children learned by moving about freely, by interacting with the Montessori materials and with each other. The accelerated learning for which Montessori schools were famous—children often begin reading at three and learn advanced math principles before first grade—grew out of the child's natural "inner direction." According to Montessori's philosophy, genuine learning didn't happen because of pushy teachers or pressuring parents.

It happened because of the nature of the child and the design of her "prepared environment."

In any event, in the early sixties, American soil was ready. The seeds of early childhood education took hold and blossomed in this country in an unprecedented way. In addition to the growing obsession with academic achievement among the educated and affluent, there was another factor that boosted not only early education but parent education. President Lyndon B. Johnson's War on Poverty in the early sixties brought us federally funded Head Start programs to prepare children of the inner city and economically depressed rural areas for school. In an attempt to strengthen families and communities, parent involvement was a requirement in the Head Start program. A basic principle of Head Start was that the community must be part of the process of educating children. Now we say, "It takes a village." Mothers and grandmothers volunteered in the classroom, just the way middle-class mothers did in private co-op nursery schools.

It was in this era—the sixties and early seventies—that I raised my children and turned my attention to child development professionally. First I trained as a Montessori teacher, then I became child development supervisor for the Catholic Archdiocese of Los Angeles, where I was responsible for establishing twelve Head Start programs. I later taught child development classes in our local community college: Child, Family, and Community and Art for Teachers of Young Children.

But it was Head Start—in the wake of the Watts riots during the summer of 1965—that I remember most vividly. Celia and Aleta were both attending a Montessori school in the suburbs by that time. During the summer months, the girls accompanied me on supervision visits to my modified Montessori Head Start classrooms in east and south central Los Angeles, Compton, and Watts. My daughters felt completely at home in these child development centers, playing with black and Hispanic children from war-torn streets. The ground rules and classroom design were the same as at the Montessori school they went to, and the materials were very similar. In fact, my kids said they preferred the Head Start classrooms because there were more art activities. When I saw their reaction, I knew I had achieved my goal of bringing the same education affluent children were getting (for a very high tuition, I might add) to children whose families could never have afforded it.

After several successful years in Head Start, my husband and I opened an educational toy design company. Then personal tragedy struck. My father began suffering bouts of mental illness, and my parents separated after thirty-five years together, followed by the abrupt end of my own ten-year marriage and the dissolution of our business partnership. In a matter of months, my entire world came crashing down around me. I was suddenly faced with single parenting, relocating to a new community, rebuilding my career as a designer and an education consultant, and figuring out what to do with the rest of my life.

At this time, it was my good fortune to hear Dr. Thomas Gordon speak at a national Montessori conference. I was struggling with finding my own style of parenting now that I was single, and Dr. Gordon's words were like balm for my weary soul. Communication was the key, he was saying. Learn to listen to the feelings and needs of others. Facilitate others to solve their own problems. Make your own feelings and needs known to others. Let others know how their actions impact you. Solve problems creatively as a family. Accept differences in values. He offered techniques for applying these principles in everyday life. Dr. Gordon's book, *Parent Effectiveness Training*, helped me in all my relationships, not only with my children but with friends and coworkers, too. I went on to receive instructor certification in Gordon's P.E.T. and T.E.T. (Teacher Effectiveness Training) programs and taught parents, teachers, and school administrators.

As I got in touch with my feelings through applying Gordon's methods, my customary coping mechanism of taking on too much responsibility started to break down. I became ill. Or more accurately, I surrendered to a sickness of body and soul that I had harbored for a long time. The sheer effort of coping with all the dramatic changes since my divorce three years before had caught up with me. My body wouldn't function as usual, and I had to go to bed. I'm eternally grateful to my mother for helping with the girls during this time.

The illness turned out to be a blessing in disguise. Utterly exhausted and baffled by the fact that the doctors could neither diagnose nor treat my malady, I feared I was going to die. In my desperation, I began keeping a journal of my inner life. Feelings, thoughts, dreams, and wishes came pouring out on the pages of my artist's sketch pads. At the same time, I was reading the first volumes of Anaïs Nin's *Diary* and also an illustrated book by Swiss psychologist Carl Jung, *Man and His Symbols*. The images and symbols in the Jung book inspired me to draw my feelings and dreams in what I later realized was a journal. I also stumbled onto another revelation—that writing with the nondominant hand had great healing powers. These discoveries led me to the discovery of my life's work: the Creative Journal and expressive arts therapy.

It was this creative process of drawing and writing in my journal along with holistic medical treatment (acupressure massage, preventive medicine, and psychotherapy) that led to my complete recovery without medication. (I later learned that I had been struggling with a condition similar to lupus that affects the collagen, or connective tissue of the body. I had "come unglued," physically and emotionally.)

This method of exploring the inner life, which I later called the Creative Journal Method, led to a new career as an art therapist, a workshop leader, and eventually the author of many self-help books. In view of my previous careers in both art and child development, it is no accident that I pioneered Inner Child healing and Inner Family work in my private practice as an art therapist in the late seventies. I took what I already knew about family dynamics and simply applied it to the individual psyche. It was the discovery of my own Inner Child and reparenting myself through Inner Family work that turned my illness around. My emotional, spontaneous, intuitive, and natural self wanted me to embrace her and be her loving and protective parent. As I reparented that vulnerable and wounded child within (who had been traumatized by crisis and tragedy), I came back to life and found a reason to go on living. The healing power of art and writing called to me and showed me the way back to personal joy and service to others.

I share this story because I want you to know that I have been there and back. As a mother, I have been to the depths and also to the ecstatic heights of what parenting has to offer. I have shared parenthood as half of a couple, been a single parent, and been the parent of stepchildren in a blended family. Today, as a grandparent, I can look back with the wisdom that only age and experience can bring and share this tool—the Creative Journal. May your journey into parenting bring you as much life and love as it has me. You deserve the best. And so do your children and their children and all the children after them.

Getting Ready

I

Becoming a Parent

Taking on the role of parent is perhaps the most awesome adventure on which one can embark. Like life, parenthood is filled with everything you can imagine, only more so. It takes us to highs and lows, agony and ecstasy, crisis and opportunity. I know of no other undertaking that demands more and guarantees less. That is not to say that there are not rich rewards—the first smile of your infant, a hug from a toddler, the birthday card made by your preschooler, your youngster's proud victories in the arts, sports, or academic achievement. One thing you can count on is the unexpected. There simply are no assurances that anything will turn out the way you expected or wanted it to.

For that reason, parenting is one of the most arduous of spiritual practices. It shakes you loose from old ideas and habits, presents you constantly with challenges to your isolated ego-self, who wants to control and predict and look good in the eyes of others. Parenting invites you to grow up (in the best sense of the term) while honoring the *child-spirit* in yourself and in your child. Parenting is the best school of psychology I know. It is a superb training ground for teaching, nursing, business (especially management and negotiations), and a host of other careers. Ask any working mom or full-time dad. Parenting is the advanced course in the school of life. Sign up with care. You're in for a wild ride.

OUR CHILDREN: WHAT THEY ARE AND WHAT THEY AREN'T

One thing a parent learns early on is that children have a life of their own. As Kahlil Gibran cautions in his spiritual guide to life, *The Prophet,* our children are not our possessions. They come through us and we are here to help them, but we cannot direct their destiny. That is in the hands of a power greater than ourselves. Our children are with us for our safekeeping, guidance, and love. They are with us for a very short time.

Now that I am a grandmother, I see just how short a time it is. As a young mother buried under piles of diapers and baby bottles, waking up at all hours for nocturnal feedings, I didn't see how fleeting the time was. When I was carpooling kids to school halfway across Los Angeles on congested freeways while juggling career and single-parenting, I had no clue how quickly the years would pass. Yet I did have a sense that these were precious times and that parenting was to be appreciated for the incomparable lessons and opportunities it presented. In that, I have never been disappointed. Tested, yes. Disappointed, no.

Children are incredible teachers. That is not to say that we are not our children's teachers, too. It just means that it's a two-way street. We learn from them as they learn from us. The very act of becoming a parent (by birth, adoption, marriage, or however we wind up with that role) challenges us to learn. Soon we find ourselves learning what parenting means to *us*. What *we* value. How we see ourselves. What our limits and boundaries are. What aspirations and dreams we hold. It all comes out in the open when we take on this formidable task of parenting another human being. I can guarantee that if you let it, parenting will provide you with opportunities for growth that you never dreamed possible.

EMBRACING PARENTING

In order to reap the deepest rewards available to you, it is important to embrace parenting with all your might. Reach out and hug it with both arms. Fall in love with your own unique style of being a parent and find your own true self. For on the road to becoming the parent you were meant to be, you will find the person you were meant to be as well.

How can I do this? you might be asking. How can I find my own way of being a parent? There are so many theories, methods, and opinions about raising children. Add to that all the differences in cultural child-rearing styles and you can end up in a morass of confusion. Obviously parenting is not for the faint of heart. Clearly it is a demanding job and a huge responsibility. How do I do it? What experts do I listen to? Whose advice should I seek? Where are my role models? These are all good questions.

THE ANSWERS LIE WITHIN

In the chapters that follow, you will explore all these questions and more. And where will the answers come from? Not from me and not from your mother or mother-in-law or Aunt Sadie. And not from the experts (many of whom disagree with each other on the "right way" to raise a child). No, the answers will come from you. From the "still, small voice within," the part of you that contains wisdom and guidance for being an authentic, creative parent to your child. You've heard this before, and you'll hear it again: the truth is within you. The world's great spiritual leaders have taught this. You can find it in any number of scriptures from all cultures and traditions. All you need to do is apply it to parenting.

Now this is no small task, finding the truth within. Yet there are ways to do it. And that is what this book is really about. In fact, it's what *all* my books are about. For I received the gift of Creative Journaling from my own Inner Self during that bleak time when a life-threatening illness was sapping my energy and will to live. My journal was a flashlight during my "dark night of the soul." It was the thing that saved my life. And now I pass it along to you.

WHAT IS CREATIVE JOURNALING?

Creative Journaling is a method of journal-keeping using both words and pictures (drawing, doodling, photo collage). In addition, it features writing and drawing with both the dominant hand (the one you normally write with) and the nondominant hand (the hand you do *not* usually write with). My twenty-five years of research have shown that writing and drawing with your nondominant hand allow more ready access to feelings, visual thinking, original insights, and inner wisdom. Why is this so?

It has long been known that the brain is divided into two hemispheres, with each half specializing in certain functions. Research in the last three decades has shown that the left hemisphere is adept at verbal and mathematical processes, sequential logic, and rational thought. We use it to make schedules, pay bills, follow verbal instructions, and so on. Our school systems rely heavily on left-brain learning and thinking.

The little-used right brain has not received much attention until recently. It contains centers that govern intuitive knowing, visual-spatial perception, emotional expressiveness, and breakthrough thinking. These are all nonrational, nonverbal functions. Artists and inventors are adept at using the right brain, as are individuals with highly developed interpersonal skills. The right brain's gifts to us are visual imagery, kinesthetic and sensory awareness, emotional expressiveness, poetic thought, and metaphoric and holistic thinking (seeing the "big picture"). The "Aha!" moment when we discover a new solution or an invention is a right-brain phenomenon. The right brain is readily accessed through the arts (which have always been the stepchild in school curriculum budgets), meditation, and using the nondominant hand for drawing and writing.

It may simply be that the hand that was not taught to write is free to express from the nonverbal, nonlinear areas of the brain. According to leading scientists who have commented on my work, such as Roger Sperry (winner of a Nobel Prize for brain research) and Dr. Valerie Hunt (former researcher in kinesiology at UCLA), by writing and drawing with the nondominant hand, you are accessing the right hemisphere of the brain. Your nondominant hand may not be able to write very well, like its literate partner (your dominant hand), but it has ready access to those functions that make creativity and human communication possible at the deepest level.

The Creative Journal Method does not disregard the left, more verbal side of the brain. It just puts right-brain visual, emotional, and intuitive processing first and then follows up with more left-brain reflective writing. In this way, we access both sides of the brain and put them in communication with each other. I like to refer to this as "letting the left brain know what the right brain is doing." (The physical hemispheres associated with the different types of thinking actually vary with the individual, with exceptions to the more common "cross-wired" configuration in both right- and left-handed groups. If you'd like more information about my research and more in-depth activities for integrating the brain hemispheres, let me suggest my book *The Power of Your Other Hand.*)

In the examples given in this book:

> writing in the dominant hand appears like this

> **writing in the nondominant hand appears like this**

Creative Journaling is for *self-discovery through art and writing.* You need no special talent or training in art or writing in order to express yourself in these forms. You are not being asked to make Art or to perform. I know of no better way to access the natural, spontaneous child within the adult than these creative activities. You can observe this for yourself if you watch kids. Little children don't complain that they have no talent or artistic ability. They love to paint and draw (and play with clay and Play-Doh and finger paints and all manner of art materials). That's all I'm asking you to do. Be a kid again. Play with the materials. Don't judge yourself. Stop striving for perfection or approval. Your Creative Journal is only for your eyes. So relax and have fun.

BENEFITS OF CREATIVE JOURNALING

The Creative Journal can help you:

- Get in touch with your true feelings and needs
- Express your feelings and needs to yourself (and eventually to others)

- Explore and reflect on your beliefs and values regarding family life
- Learn to nurture and protect your Inner Child (emotional, physical, and creative needs)
- Reframe negative past experiences so you can learn from them
- Change negative beliefs into more supportive ones
- Discover and appreciate your own innate creativity
- Discover and appreciate your child's creativity
- Treasure the sacred moments of parenting
- Understand your own style of parenting
- Celebrate your family and your unique relationship with your child
- Learn ways to play with and enjoy the gift of parenting your child
- Gain wisdom and insights from your own experiences as a parent
- Celebrate the uniqueness of your child (or each of your children)

GUIDELINES FOR CREATIVE JOURNALING

Each journal activity in this book has a title, list of materials, and purpose. There are simple steps for how to do these activities. I suggest reading the book through first and then concentrating on the chapters that are most relevant for you. Go back and reread your selected chapters in the sequence in which they appear; do the journal activities in the order in which they are given. After you've done the journal assignments once, there are many activities that you may want to do over and over again. That's fine. Choose the ones that are most appropriate to your needs at any given time.

There are examples from the Creative Journals of other parents to stimulate your imagination and to share the experience, strength, and hope of others. These examples are not meant to be imitated or copied. *There is no right or wrong way to do Creative Journaling. Only your way.* So please don't compare your work to anyone else's. This is about finding your own unique voice with which to express yourself. Explore with line, shape, and color. Discover your own personal symbols and images. Play with words and find new meaning in your life.

WHEN TO WORK IN YOUR JOURNAL

You don't have to use your journal every day. Of course, the more you write and draw in your Creative Journal, the more you are apt to gain from it. But don't make it into "spinach" that you *have to eat* or "homework" that you *have to do or else*. You'll just criticize yourself for failing, feel guilty, and then resist and rebel against the whole process. Please guard against this. I don't care whether you keep a Creative Journal or not. The tools are here if you want them. (By the way, I bought my first blank book at age fifteen and didn't write a word in it until I was thirty-five. Talk about a slow start. So who am I to judge anyone else for not starting a journal right away?)

Do your best to set aside journal time for yourself when you are ready to do it. You may find that a certain time of day is best for you. Perhaps bedtime (after your family is asleep) or in the early morning (before everyone is up). Making a regular appointment with yourself can help get you into the "journal habit." It's also a great way for you to carve out a little time just for yourself. Busy mothers have told me that this was the biggest benefit from Creative Journaling: *taking quality time out for themselves.* You can put the Creative Journal on your calendar to remind yourself, just as you do with other appointments. This is especially important for parents who tend to put everyone else first and themselves last.

Fit journaling into your everyday life in the way that works best for you. Be creative. Be unique. Be practical.

KEEPING TRACK

Date the first page of every entry and keep your entries in chronological order. This will be helpful in looking back (which is part of the method) and reviewing where you've traveled in your inner life. I recommend a bound blank book or three-ring binder (see the list of materials later in the chapter). Whatever you use, keep your work in the sequence in which you did it.

PRIVACY AND CONFIDENTIALITY

Journaling is a form of self-therapy. And like all therapy and counseling, it needs to be confidential. This ensures honesty and spontaneity. If you are worried about others seeing your journal or what they will think of what you draw and write, it will be impossible for you to be truthful with yourself. And that is the essence of Creative Journaling. Without a commitment to the truth, you might as well throw your journal out the window. So safeguard your work and yourself by keeping your journal in a safe place away from the eyes of others. If you wish to share a selection of your work with a trusted person—like your significant other, therapist, or spiritual counselor—by all means do so. Just be sure that you do not share it with anyone who is critical of you. Protect yourself from people who think they know better than you what you ought to feel or say or do with your life. Remember, on the subject of your own life, *you* are the expert. If you ever had any doubts about that, hopefully Creative Journaling will dispel them.

In line with the confidentiality factor is the need to have as much privacy as possible when you are doing your journal work. If there are lots of interruptions, it's difficult to go inside and explore your inner world. There will be more about setting the mood for fruitful journaling when we begin the activities.

I would like to say, however, that sometimes our feelings won't wait. You can take your journal with you and turn to it when you're "killing time" in the doctor's waiting room or riding on public transportation or waiting for any event or meeting to get under way. Just make sure to keep your journal work confidential, no matter where you are.

MATERIALS FOR CREATIVE JOURNALING

1. JOURNAL

A blank book, preferably hardbound with unlined white paper (8½″ × 11″ or larger)

OR

A three-ring binder with lots of unlined white paper (same size as above)

2. DRAWING AND WRITING MATERIALS

Felt pens for writing in twelve or more assorted colors (nontoxic)

Crayons or fat felt markers for drawing (twelve colors or more)

Optional: colored pencils or oil or chalk pastels (*Note:* If you use a fixative spray for pastel to prevent it from smearing, use one that is nontoxic.)

3. COLLAGE MATERIALS

Magazines with pictures of families and other topics suggested in collage assignments in exercises throughout this book

Scissors

Glue (white glue or glue stick)

Drawing paper or poster board (preferably 18″ × 24″)

Note: Collages can also be done in your journal.

PREPARING TO WORK IN YOUR JOURNAL

Creativity flows more naturally when you are in the right frame of mind (or brain, as the case may be). Before doing journal work, one way to prepare yourself is to create a special place for yourself that is your "journal corner." Like a meditation room or temple, a journal corner is the place where you regularly engage in introspection. If you do journaling in the same spot, your mind and body will take the cue as soon as you sit down there. The quiet mood of introspection will come over you automatically. It's the same principle that is at work for meditators or people who pray or practice an instrument or paint. Their meditation room or temple or studio becomes invested with the intention and the grace of repeated practice in that place.

I like to do journal work in bed before going to sleep. When I work in my journal during the daytime, I sit in a special chair in my meditation room. It is very easy for me to go inside and explore feelings, thoughts, experiences, wishes, and dreams when I am in these locations. They are private, quiet, and beautiful corners for refuge and retreat, my special places. They nourish me and allow me to be alone with myself in a way that restores and rejuvenates me. Find your place. Go there and roam. There is a universe inside you waiting to be explored.

Another wonderful way to prepare for journaling is to get centered in your body. The following "journey through your body" only takes a few minutes, but the benefits are tremendous. This relaxation meditation can do wonders in and of itself. Many journalers tell me that even if they can't find a place or time to work in their journals, they do this meditation. It has helped them immeasurably when things have become chaotic and tense.

Grounding and Centering

Place: A quiet spot where you can be alone without interruptions

Purpose: To relax your body and mind; to let go of worries and extraneous thoughts; to practice being in the here and now

Activity:
1. Close your eyes and do some natural deep breathing. Don't force the breath. Just open to it. Slowly inhale and exhale, allowing your breathing to become progressively slower and more rhythmic. Experience your breath as the nourishing gift of life that it is. Be receptive to it and thank the Creator (your Higher Power or whatever you call the spirit of all creation) for the breath of life.
2. Now focus your attention on the feelings in your body. Are there any areas of tension, or do you feel any pain? Do an inventory of your body. Start at the bottom of your feet and work your way up. Check out each area of your body. Focus on one foot and leg and then the other. Then

become aware of your torso and internal organs. Then move up to your neck and shoulders, one arm and then the other. And finish by being aware of all the sensations in your face and jaw, ears and back of your head, and the crown of your head.

3. Go back to any areas where you experienced pain or discomfort and imagine that you are sending the breath to them. Let each of these areas be receptive to the breath of life. Let the tension melt away and the energy return to each of these areas. As you do this, say to yourself, "My [body part] is feeling very relaxed."

4. When you are through with your body inventory and relaxation, repeat to yourself, "My body is feeling very relaxed. I am loved."

5. When you feel ready, open your eyes.

Another wonderful way to relax is by scribbling or doodling. This exercise has been very effective in stress reduction workshops for busy adults who feel burdened by professional and family responsibilities. It's a wonderful way to lighten up and be a kid again.

Dances on Paper

Materials: Journal and felt pens or crayons; a tape or CD of your favorite music

Purpose: To relax through rhythmic drawing to music; to use playful activity as a stress reduction technique

Activity:

1. Put on your favorite music and begin doodling and scribbling to the music, using your *dominant* hand. Imagine that you are an ice skater and are leaving the pattern of your movements on the ice. Only in this case, the skating rink is your paper. Or simply imagine that you are dancing on the paper. Don't try to draw a picture of anything.

This is not about making Art. It's about being a little kid again and scribbling just the way children do.

2. Now switch and draw with the other (*nondominant*) hand for a while. How does it feel? Awkward and slow? Or relaxing and fun? Observe your feelings and physical response to this kind of drawing.

3. Next, put a pen or crayon in each hand and draw with *both hands at the same time*. Have a duet with yourself. What happens? Do your hands imitate each other? Or does each of your hands have a mind of its own?

Congratulations. You have just begun the great adventure of Creative Journaling. Welcome aboard!

2

Making Room for Parenting

This chapter is about making room in your mind and heart for being the kind of parent *you* want to be. It includes some tools for sorting through the beliefs, values, and child-rearing practices that were handed down to you. In short, you'll be doing some mental and emotional "spring cleaning."

FAMILY VALUES AND YOU

Have you ever consciously thought about the values and rules you grew up with? Which ones do you still hold to? Have you arrived at any values of your own that differ from those of your family of origin? What values do you want to share with your child? These are all very important questions for finding a style of parenting that works for you.

In the controversy over "family values," we often lose sight of the fact that every family has values. Values are simply the things that we honor. How do we know what our values are? By what we *do,* by the amount of time and energy we devote to what we hold important. For example, the Ramirez family considers their community of great importance. They are active in a coalition for inner-city safety and improvement. Both parents and all three children were instrumental in helping to build a pocket park and playground for their neighborhood.

Joellen Smith, a single parent, believes in entrepreneurship and invests much of her energy and time in running her small framing business. She also values time with her family. During the summer months, Joellen takes her two teenagers to work with her and is training them to frame pictures and do book-keeping. The kids are following in Mom's entrepreneurial foot-steps as they earn their own money and learn job skills.

The Washingtons value their religion, and the family devotes most of the weekend to church activities. Mrs. Washington is a piano teacher, and her children have inherited her love of music. They play several instruments and perform for fund-raisers and at parties.

Dan Chang, a textile importer, has been a world traveler since childhood, when his parents took him on many trips abroad. He shares his love of different cultures with his new bride, Mari-anne, a travel agent who especially enjoys foreign lands and exotic architecture. They are planning vacations to Africa and Asia for themselves and Marianne's two sons from her previous marriage.

THE RULES YOU LIVE BY

Values provide the structure for societies and religions. Group values have a way of getting translated into laws and moral precepts. In addition, each culture passes down generally ac-cepted customs and traditions with their own set of informal rules. There's no law that says you have to have turkey on Thanksgiving, but a vast majority of Americans do. Why? "TRA-DI-TION" (to quote Tevye from *Fiddler on the Roof*). Customs are so ingrained that many families even fight over them. For instance, if someone wants to tamper with a long-held holiday tradition (change the menu, the location of the gathering, or—worse yet—ignore it altogether), a huge row can easily ensue. Some factions will argue for "the way we've al-ways done it," whereas others would just as soon forget the whole thing. As one of my friends declared when I asked her what she was doing for Christmas, "Me? I'm gonna get out of Dodge. In our family, Christmas is a war zone, with everybody wanting to do it *their* way. I think I'll go to Hawaii this year. That will be far enough away." We all have stories in our familial closet about "the most horrible holiday."

Whether they be civic, religious, cultural, or familial, values always translate into the rules we live by. Breaking society's rules as encoded in laws normally leads to consequences. Ignoring civic or federal statutes can lead to fines or even imprisonment. Exceed the speed limit and you're likely to get a traffic citation. Organizations and clubs structure their rules as bylaws. For example, if you neglect paying dues, your membership lapses. Employers have their own sets of rules that influence hiring and firing policies as well as performance reviews.

As the basic unit of society, each family has its own values and therefore its own rules. You may be wondering how you can consciously create values for your own family. It's simple: pay attention to what you genuinely feel is important. Instead of automatically adopting someone else's family rules or blindly following a one-size-fits-all definition of "family values" and "healthy parenting," ask yourself: What is really important to me as an individual? To me and my family? What values do I want to share with my child? Do I walk my talk? Do I practice what I preach?

The important things to ask about any custom, tradition, or rule are: Does it still make sense? Is it useful today, or is it obsolete? A custom that made sense in past situations may be irrelevant now. Do your personal rules and customs reflect your true values? Children learn from what *we do,* not from what we say *they should do.* When they grow up, they can and will choose their own values. Until then, we owe it to them (and to ourselves) to get clear about our values and to let our values shape the rules we actually live by from day to day. For a world without consciously chosen, heartfelt values is a world without a center of gravity. It is a world without love and respect. In this chapter, you'll be developing greater awareness of your values so that you can set priorities and make choices more thoughtfully, especially when it comes to parenting.

CHILD-REARING METHODS AND YOU

In the cultural melting pot that is America, *there is no single way to raise children.* You can choose and decide for yourself. In fact, you are expected to. However, there are so many theories and methods of child rearing that it can be downright baffling. You may browse around and encounter some theories, opinions, and handy hints for raising your child. If you encounter one that appears to have merit, I suggest you test it out for yourself, the way I did Montessori's theories. Use your home as a laboratory and your child as the subject of observation. If your firsthand experience proves a particular theory or method, then take it to heart. If not, forget it. As a newly single parent, I applied Tom Gordon's Parent Effectiveness Training with my own children and found that it worked. We solved problems more creatively, and my daughters became more responsible. If Gordon's method hadn't worked with our family, I would have dropped it.

In addition to the methods espoused by professionals, there are also lots of amateurs who will be all too eager to share their child-rearing theories with you. As one young mother observed, "Have you ever noticed how, when someone has a baby or adopts a child, everyone suddenly becomes an 'expert'? I guess they're well intended, but a lot of these people who are dishing out advice to me have never had a child or raised one. Yet they know how it 'ought to be done' and are the first to tell you."

Comments like this always remind me of my Grandma Grace. After her husband died, leaving her with four children to raise, three meddling sisters-in-law came to pay a visit. They proceeded to tell the young widow how to raise her family. Although she was a soft-spoken immigrant woman, I'm told Grandma had no trouble taking a stand. Fiercely protective of her kids, she declared, "These are *my* children. I have raised them this long, and I will continue raising them—as *I* see fit." End of subject. Grandma spoke little English at the time, and it was the beginning of the Great Depression. She had to raise her children single-handedly, taking in work as a seamstress (a trade for which she'd been trained in Italy). She did a great job with both of these formidable tasks!

THE SCHOOL OF LIFE

Child-rearing theories and opinions aside, when it comes to discovering your own way of being a parent, reality is the best teacher. It is in facing everyday challenges and making choices that our own values take shape. This process usually starts with questions. A pregnant woman wonders, "Should I breast-feed or bottle-feed my baby?" A new mother asks, "Is it healthy for me and the baby if I go back to work right away, or should I wait?" A young father wonders, "My father used to spank me, but I don't feel good when I hit my kids. What should I do?" A couple deliberates, "We can't conceive a baby. Should we look into adoption?"

When asking such questions, you can do one of two things: (1) seek answers from others and try to apply them to yourself or (2) gather information, take time to discover your true feelings and needs, and then decide what works for you and your family.

As to the first approach, my observation is that each family is unique and what works for one may not work for another. I often encounter parents who have run from book to book, from expert to expert, searching for answers. Many of them become utterly confused because they find that the experts sometimes disagree with each other. To make it worse, their generalized answers frequently miss the mark. These parents are still in the dark about what to do with *their* child in specific problem situations.

When my child development students used to ask me which expert had the answers to child rearing, I often asked a question in return: "Of the authors you've been reading, which one do you think ever changed a diaper or dealt with an active two-year-old in the supermarket? I'd want to see those kinds of credentials before I took their advice too seriously."

Now I'm not saying to disregard what professionals have to say about thumb-sucking or bed-wetting or hyperactivity or any number of behaviors that are worthy of parental concern. Get all the information you can from knowledgeable and experienced sources in your community or outside of it. Just remember that although others may offer useful advice, they don't carry the responsibility for parenting your child day to day. The decisions and actions are up to you. Blindly imitating their solutions or comparing yourself to them can get you further and further away from your greatest resource: your own personal experience and your innate wisdom.

I learned this as a young parent when my girls were very small. They are fifteen months apart, so at the time Aleta was an infant and Celia was barely walking. One afternoon while I was taking diapers out of the dryer and ironing my husband's shirts, a former schoolmate dropped in with her three children in tow. Considering herself an expert, she chided me because my oldest wasn't fully potty-trained yet. She let me know that her youngest had been trained since she was half Celia's age. At first, I felt guilty and inadequate. "Maybe she's right," I thought. "Maybe Celia *should* be potty-trained by now. I'm probably doing it all wrong. I'll have to look it up in Dr. Spock." (Benjamin Spock was *the* child-rearing guru of the sixties.)

I read Spock but couldn't see how Celia's life would be ruined by not being potty-trained yet. Then I gave it some more thought. Memories came back. I could hear my mother's voice comparing me to a neighbor girl who made better grades than I did. I remembered how I *hated* it when Mom did that. In fact, I used to defend myself by saying, "Yeah, but she doesn't write music like I do, or play the piano or draw pretty pictures like mine, either." Early on, I had been labeled a "talented child" by my teachers (meaning abilities in the arts), but I was definitely not a straight-A student. When my mother played the deadly "comparison game," she was focusing on academic subjects, which frankly left me cold, instead of appreciating me for what I loved and did well.

The more I reflected on those incidents with my mother, the more I knew I couldn't pressure my child to perform according to anyone else's expectations. I stopped worrying about it, and Celia was potty-trained when she was good and ready. Many years later, Celia quit college after one year because she was bored. I wasn't upset about it, as some family members were. I had learned long before that she (like all children) had her own timetable for learning different things. She preferred the school of life over the University of California. Why was I not surprised?

As you've probably guessed by now, my vote goes to the second approach to parenting: gathering information and then finding your own style of raising your child. By all means, be informed. Read books, attend lectures and courses, join support groups, talk to professionals, but be true to yourself and your child.

Most important, *listen to your child.* Take your cues from what he or she needs and is communicating to you. Make it a point to pay attention to your child's body language, emotional expression, daily routines, changes in behavior. Much of this is nonverbal in the early years, and so you will need to learn the language of the child, *your* child. For all children are different. Each one has a unique way of communicating. Observe your child's actions and gestures, facial expressions, and verbal expression through sounds (and later through words). I have full confidence that you can do this, that you can learn the language of the child, *your* child.

In the exercises that follow, you'll be developing greater awareness of yourself and your loved ones. Everyday challenges will present themselves to you. As you continue with this practice of self-reflection, you'll be *journaling your way into the answers that work for you.*

REFLECTING ON BEING A PARENT

Journal-keeping can be an immensely helpful way to become more thoughtful and aware of how you are parenting your child. The journal is a wonderful place to sort through your values, questions, observations, and needs. It is also a great vehicle for clearing feelings from the past so that you can move forward and find your own way into parenthood.

What Parenting Means to Me

Materials: Journal and felt pens

Purpose: To reflect upon your own beliefs, expectations, and
              feelings about being a parent

Activity:

1. With your *dominant* hand, write the word *Parent* at the top left corner of your journal page. Then free-associate by making a list of words that relate to the word *Parent*. Do not plan what you write or think about it. Write as quickly as you can and avoid deliberating on or judging anything you write. Keep listing words until you feel finished.

2. Read over your list of words from step 1. On the next page of your journal, do some freewriting on the theme "What parenting means to me." Again, use your *dominant* hand. Write quickly, without making corrections or in any way editing your comments. This time, write in sentences or phrases.

3. Continue using your *dominant* hand and make a list titled "My Expectations as a Parent."

4. This time, use your *nondominant* hand and answer the question "What scares me about being a parent?" When you have finished, write about "What excites me about being a parent?"

5. Continuing with your *nondominant* hand, complete the following sentence as often as you like: "I'd like to be the kind of parent who . . ." Or, if you like, express this in a drawing—again, using your *nondominant* hand.

Parent

responsible   respectable
supportive   huggable
love   cooperative
caring   understanding
worrisome   playful
tired   nice

What parenting means to me:

Parenting means to me to raise my child to the best of my knowledge. To teach her right from wrong. To give her a good model or be a good role model for her. I believe . . . I need to give her much loving, responsibility, understanding, and a cooperative, supportive environment.

I need to be very, very patient!

What scares me about being a parent:
1. My daughter meeting bad influences in school
2. My patience running out
3. Not teaching my child enough before junior high
4. Making sure she's eating the right food

What excites me about being a parent:
1. My daughter is very smart.
2. She is creative.
3. She is very sociable.
4. I get very good compliments.
5. My daughter asks a million questions.

HOW YOU WERE RAISED

Getting clarity about how you were raised can help you develop your own style of parenting. The next set of exercises will help you take a good, honest look at the past and get a clearer picture of where you want to go. You'll explore your beliefs and assumptions and revisit the cherished memories and challenges of your own childhood. From this complex tapestry, you'll be able to pull out the threads that seem most valuable and weave them into a new pattern.

Return to Childhood

Materials: Journal and felt pens; optional: family photos from childhood showing you and your parents or guardians and other family members

Purpose: To gain insights about the values of your family of origin

Activity:

1. If you have any photos of your family taken when you were a child or teenager, get them out and look at them. Select one picture that speaks to you. With your *nondominant* hand, answer the following questions: Who is in the picture? What was going on at the time the picture was taken? If each person in the picture could talk, what would he or she say? What is important to each person who appears in this photo, including yourself? Are any pets in the picture? What would the pet(s) say about your family?

2. Using your *nondominant* hand, draw a scene that you recall from childhood. Choose a scene that includes you and family members or guardians. Stick figures are fine if you don't feel you can draw people representationally.

3. Look at the picture you just drew. With your *nondominant* hand, write about it (as suggested in step 1). Briefly describe what's going on in the picture and what each per-

son in the picture says. What is important to each of the people portrayed, including yourself?

In this picture, I'm seven. It is Sunday because Daddy is home. We're raking leaves together. When we get a real big pile, we'll burn them. I love the sound of the leaves and the smell of the fire. I love being with Daddy. I love doing things outdoors with him. I don't think we talk much. Isn't that nice? I am happy with him. I love Sunday. I love Daddy. Daddy doesn't say it, but look at him. I know he is loving. He loves me. This is a happy-day picture.

VALUES AND RULES

Each family has its own set of rules, which are driven by what it values. Some rules are stated openly. For instance, parents

who value education will encourage their children to study and set penalties if they don't. "No television until your homework is done." "No basketball until your grades have improved."

Other values may not be spoken about or encoded in formal rules, but they are modeled through the parents' actions. For instance, parents who love reading usually have lots of books in the house and set an example through their enjoyment of reading. They tend to read to their children, take them to the library, and give them books for their birthday or other occasions. The message is: "Books are wonderful. They are full of adventure, exciting information, stories, and so forth. Reading is fun." Today, many children are being raised in households where computers play the same role as books once did. That is the case in my daughter Aleta's home. As a young adult, she was hooked on computers the first time she sat down at the keyboard. She's now a programmer and has guided her four boys in computer literacy from a very early age. Why? Because she *loves* computers. In fact, it was her son Arie who (at the ripe old age of seven) introduced me to "Myst." Although I'd had a computer since before he was born, he showed me the exciting potential of interactive multimedia. No amount of parental preaching about the benefits of computer literacy can communicate as well as a genuine love of the medium can.

How I Was Raised

Materials: Journal and felt pens

Purpose: To examine the beliefs and expectations of your parents or guardians about child rearing when you were growing up

Activity:

1. With your *nondominant* hand, write the word *Rules* at the top of your journal page. Then make a list of the most important household rules you had to obey (both spoken and unspoken) when you were growing up. What was expected of you? What behavior was praised or rewarded? What was forbidden? What were the consequences for breaking the family rules?

   Note: If you lived in more than one household, or with different parents or guardians, select the household(s) that made the biggest impression on you.

2. With your *nondominant* hand, draw a picture showing things that were valued in your family of origin. Use pictorial shorthand and create symbols such as $ for money, musical notes for music, a football or tennis racket or some other appropriate symbol for sports.

3. With your *dominant* hand, on the next page in your journal write down the messages that you got from your parents or guardians about what was important in life.

4. Look at your picture again and then read what you just wrote in step 3. Do you genuinely value any of the things your family of origin thought were important? Are there things you do not value? Write about them using your *dominant* hand.

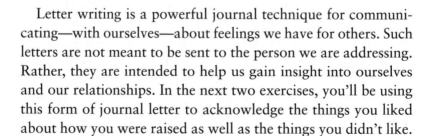

Rules

1. Do not speak when adults are speaking.
2. Do not say anything that would worry Mom and Dad or make them feel bad.
3. Do not tell family "secrets."
4. Do not cry.
5. Do not quit anything you start.
6. Do not ask questions.
7. Eat everything on your plate.
8. Be good in school but not too smart.
9. Be quiet.
10. Don't talk to strangers.
11. Don't get near dogs or cats.

What were the messages I got about what is important in life?

Don't show anybody anything but a sweet, nice, normal reflection of your family. No temper, no sadness, nothing to draw attention to yourself. Be what you think others would like you to be, even if it doesn't "fit you." Be responsible for others. If you make a mistake, they will be mad or hurt.

Be a good student, but if I were to be "too smart," I wouldn't get a husband. It is important to be pretty and *not fat*. Stay away from tomboy activities and act "feminine" at all times.

Honor others at my own expense. And *be grateful* for everything I have. Be worried about the future, about money, health, new experiences. Don't take risks. Don't trust other women.

Letter writing is a powerful journal technique for communicating—with ourselves—about feelings we have for others. Such letters are not meant to be sent to the person we are addressing. Rather, they are intended to help us gain insight into ourselves and our relationships. In the next two exercises, you'll be using this form of journal letter to acknowledge the things you liked about how you were raised as well as the things you didn't like.

You'll be "giving credit where credit is due" and also being totally honest about your feelings.

Perhaps the greatest value of journal letters is that we can be completely candid. No one is going to get his or her feelings hurt or argue or defend himself or herself. You will not be interrupted by the other person's emotional reactions to what you say. Also, you can write journal letters to people who are dead, estranged, or who have disappeared from your life. This is a wonderful way to clear old feelings without using anyone else for target practice. It's safe and nonthreatening. As you write, remember that these letters are intended for your eyes only. So say what you feel and mean what you say.

Paying Tribute

Materials: Journal and felt pens

Purpose: To identify what you liked about the way your parents or guardians raised you; to express your appreciation to those who raised you

Activity:
1. With your *dominant* hand, write a letter to a parent or guardian or someone who was responsible for you when you were a child or teenager. Tell this person what you *liked* about the way he or she raised you or treated you. Express your appreciation. Do not include anything but thanks in this letter. No blaming, no litanies of grievances, no complaints. (You'll have a chance to do that later.) This is simply a "thank-you" letter.
2. With your *nondominant* hand, draw a picture of yourself with the person to whom you wrote the letter. Portray a scene that exemplifies the positive way the person raised you or related to you.

To church with my Grandmother

To my dear Grandma O'Hara:

   I want to thank you for loving me, caring for me, and feeding me when I was a baby up to about three years old. I remember when you'd take me to the Catholic church and I just felt your love. I know you loved me. Even when I was that young, I felt your loving presence. Thank you.

3. Repeat steps 1 and 2 as many times as you like, writing to and picturing a different parent or guardian each time. You may want to do this exercise for grandparents, significant aunts or uncles, or neighbors. Whoever you write to, be sure it is someone who was in a "parental role" in your life—someone who was in some way responsible for you when you were growing up.

Note: Sometimes journal-keepers decide they want to copy this thank-you letter and send it.

No childhood was happy all the time. And no parent or guardian "got it right" all the time. Parents are human, too. We all have some grievances about the times our parents hurt us, neglected us, or in some way were unable to be the loving parents we expected. So here is an opportunity to do some "spring cleaning." Dust out the cobwebs of old emotions, grudges, and resentments that really don't harm anyone but yourself. The sooner you can dump this old garbage from the past, the more prepared you will be to focus on the present and how to better parent your child today.

To Tell the Truth

Materials: Journal and felt pens, newsprint, and crayons

Purpose: To identify what you didn't like about the way you
were raised; to release old resentments toward
those who raised you

Activity:
1. With your *dominant* hand, write a journal letter to one of your parents or guardians telling what you did *not* like about the way he or she raised you. Describe the person's behavior, how it affected you then, and how it affects you now. Give some specific examples of incidents that showed the kind of child-rearing practices or behavior that you found so offensive.
2. Get your pad of newsprint paper or an old newspaper and your crayons. Then go back in time to an incident in which the person you wrote to demonstrated the behavior you disliked. Remember what happened and recall the feelings you had at the time. With your *nondominant* hand, scribble those feelings out on your paper. Use colors that express the feelings. Use as many pages of paper as you need. Really let those feelings out.
   A WORD OF CAUTION: If you had a particularly difficult childhood or experienced episodes of abuse (of any

kind), this type of anger release may bring out very power-ful emotions. *If you feel overwhelmed by your feelings at any time while doing this work, please stop.* In such cases, it is not advisable to do this process in isolation. I strongly suggest that you consider seeking professional help.

3. Using *both hands alternately,* write a dialogue with the person you wrote to in step 1. With your *dominant* hand, tell the person how you felt about the particular situation you focused on for the drawing in step 2. Then with your *nondominant* hand, let the person respond. Continue with the dialogue until you feel finished. You might want to ask why the person behaved the way he or she did. Also tell the person how the behavior affected you.

OK, Mom,

You've been dead almost four years, and I still feel scared and guilty expressing things about our relationship that both-ered me. Number 1: I was never allowed to express my hon-est feelings—I couldn't be sad or angry to you. You always compared me to other girls, and I was *never good enough!*

You found fault with just about everyone, and you'd go on and on complaining. I really resent that you taught me not to trust people. You didn't make friends easily and didn't honor the friends I made.

I felt ashamed of my feelings and learned how to hold them in and "pretend." You liked me when I pretended well. . . . You weren't open with your affection, and I always felt needy for affection, but it was hard to accept when it was offered to me. . . .

You were scared of everything. When I wanted to go out and have a new experience, I had to overcome my anxiety *and yours!* I had to do things behind your back—things I really loved and had a great time at, but I had to feel sneaky and guilty. (The price to pay for having fun!)

Well now that you have died, I *do* play—a lot! I write. I paint. I dance. I *love* my friends. I love not having to report to you.

I feel free to know myself and others. How good it feels. Finally.

Your daughter,

CLARIFYING VALUES

You've had a chance to reflect upon your own childhood. You've identified both positive and negative experiences. Now it's time to ask the big question: How do you want to parent your child? The final answers are never in on this one. For parenting, like life, is a never-ending process of confusion, discovery, insight, more confusion, and on and on. Hopefully, as your child grows, you grow as a parent and as a person. This is an important step—clarifying your own values and preferences in parenting.

Wanted: My Kind of Parent

Materials: Journal and felt pens; collage materials

Purpose: To identify and articulate your values; to shape your own style of parenting

Activity:

1. Imagine that you are your own child. You are running an ad in the classified section of the newspaper headed: "WANTED: A PARENT." With your *nondominant* hand, write a job description for this position. What qualifications does the position require? What personality traits? What experiences? What about references?

2. On the next page of your journal, with your *dominant* hand, write a letter in response to the ad. Describe what your qualifications are. What do you bring to the job? Why do you want it?

3. Create a photo collage called "Parenting." You can make this collage in your journal or on art paper or poster board (see the materials list in Chapter 1). Cut out photos from magazines that portray the kind of parenting or family experience you would like to have. Glue the pictures down in any way that feels right to you. (There is no right or wrong way to do this, so you can't possibly make a mistake.) What does your style of parenting look like?

Who is in the picture? What are they doing? How are they relating to each other? What is important to you, and how is it shown in your collage?

4. Reflect upon your collage. In your journal, with your *dominant* hand, write down your observations. What is the message of this collage about your style of parenting? About your values? About the qualities you want to cultivate in order to parent in the style you have portrayed?

Wanted: A Parent

- Someone who is happy and likes to laugh and have fun
- Someone who teaches me and doesn't get too upset if I make too much noise or do the wrong thing
- Someone who explains things and has lots of time for me
- Someone who is always going to be there and keep me safe
- Someone who appreciates who I am and what I can do
- Someone who really likes me and is proud of me
- Someone who is strong and guides me
- Someone who believes in me
- Someone whose expectations I can understand and try to meet
- Someone who will understand and accept my feelings
- Someone I can talk to

Dear child,

I would like to be a parent for someone like you, who is asking for such wonderful, genuine things. I like to play, and I could find wonderful things to do and places to go. I know how important it is for children to feel safe and cared for and to be able to express all of their feelings, no matter what they are.

As a parent, I know I would take great pride in my children, and I would help them learn many things about life. I would encourage their talents and find ways to help them discover what things they really like and what things they would really like to learn how to do. We would go places and meet people and learn about lots of interesting things.

We would talk a lot, and I would listen to your feelings and tell you more and help you understand things about people that can be confusing and hard to understand. I would love you so much and try to listen. I would do my best to help you grow up to be happy and strong. I would love you always.

3

The Inner Family

The process of becoming a parent begins long before you plan a family. It starts well before a child actually comes into your life—whether it be through giving birth, adopting, or partnering with someone who already has a child. How you feel about being a parent is deeply rooted in your own birth and childhood. Your beliefs about "how children should be raised" are shaped by how you were raised.

Many of these feelings and beliefs about parenting are unconscious, coming to the surface only when you are faced with raising a real, live flesh-and-blood child. For example, many parents (myself included) have been appalled to discover that we've said or done something we'd always vowed *never* to say or do to our own child. In a weak moment, it's easy to fall into knee-jerk reactions that come from the past.

In order to be more conscious of how you are parenting your child, you'll need to sort through the child-rearing patterns you experienced growing up and also examine your own personal needs and values. In this way, you can use what fits from the past while also finding the way that works for you and your loved ones today. And how do you do this? Through Inner Family work.

INNER FAMILY WORK

I've found that it is crucial to understand the Inner Family and the internal dynamics of how we relate to our own Inner Child. Why? Because our relationship with others is directly influenced by the Inner Family dynamic. This is especially true when we become parents. How we behave toward our children often mirrors how we were treated as children and how we treat our own Inner Child today. Whether we understand children and their needs depends heavily on our understanding of the child-spirit within us. In this chapter, I'll be leading you through an abbreviated version of my self-reparenting program.

REPARENTING YOUR INNER CHILD

The self-reparenting process recognizes that we each have within us subpersonalities that correspond to a family. There's an Inner Child, and there are Inner Parents.

The Inner Child is the emotional, physical, and intuitive part of your being. The Inner Child is alive in your body, feelings, and gut instincts. It has a deep knowing about what is safe for you, both emotionally and physically. The Inner Child also has strong spiritual sensibilities. It has faith in the invisible world and a natural ability to move between the imaginary and the physical. The Inner Child can be vulnerable and sensitive, magical and playful, or bratty and tyrannical and just like a real, honest-to-goodness child. And it never grows up and leaves home. It will always be with you. To know your Inner Child is to know yourself. A healthy Inner Child brings you energy, creativity, fun, and honesty in your relationships.

Adults who ignore their Inner Child have trouble playing, enjoying themselves, being in touch with feelings, or being spontaneous. Without an active Inner Child, such grown-ups often suffer from stress-related diseases or chronic illness because they are not aware of their physical or emotional needs. In addition, they have great difficulty relating to children and have problems with parenting. Their abandoned Inner Child resents the attention given to others and falls into what I call the Inner Child sibling rivalry syndrome. In other words, the Inner Child is angry about being neglected. When this happens, the person unconsciously vents his or her rage toward the child (or spouse or anyone else around). This anger often bursts out as harsh punishment or violence toward the child under the guise of "discipline." Pent-up rage (masquerading as parental discipline) may explode uncontrollably in the form of verbal abuse (shaming and insulting language), physical abuse, or penalties that are way out of proportion to the child's so-called misdeeds. I know of no better prevention or cure for child abuse than Inner Family work and self-reparenting on the part of adults who are raising or associated with children.

THE INNER CHILD FIRSTHAND

Since *Inner Child* became a household term in the early 1990s, many clients and workshop participants have expressed confusion about what it means. "I've heard or read about the Inner Child," they say, "but I haven't *experienced* it." Once they do my journal exercises, the confusion clears up immediately. You'll have plenty of chances to experience your Inner Child firsthand as you do the journal activities in this chapter. Let's start with a quick glimpse of your Inner Child in everyday life:

> Stop and ask yourself: When was the last time I experienced strong emotions? What feelings did I have? How did these feelings affect my body? My behavior? Did I express the feelings? How did I do that?

That "feeling self" was your Inner Child. It's as simple as that. Whether or not you expressed the feelings to anyone else, they were there all the same. Maybe you were angry and literally got hot under the collar. Or you were sad and cried (or wanted to cry). Or you got anxious about something and had nervous butterflies in your stomach. Or you were happy and laughed. Whatever the emotions, they were probably accompanied by physical sensations and even outward expression.

In this next exercise, I'd like you to express these feelings in lines, shapes, and colors on paper. This is something that little children do all the time when they scribble and doodle. This is the language of the Inner Child, too. It is direct, nonverbal, and primarily right-brain.

Unless Ye Become as Little Children

Materials: Journal and felt pens or crayons

Purpose: To experience and express the Inner Child firsthand

Activity:

1. Revisit the feelings you got in touch with in the previous paragraphs. With your *nondominant* hand, using felt pens or crayons, draw a picture of the feelings you just remembered. Don't try to make Art or portray a scene. Simply doodle, scribble, or draw abstract shapes to express the feelings. Colors are significant. Select colors that you associate with these feelings. There is no right or wrong way to do this. Your natural intuition will direct you. There is no particular way this drawing should look. Just let yourself scribble or draw the way you did when you were a little kid and see what happens.

2. Still using your *nondominant* hand, on the next page of your journal, write or print words that express the feelings in your drawing. Again, use colors that you associate with these feelings.

3. Switch the pen to your *dominant* hand. On the next page in your journal, write your reaction to the drawing and writing you just did.

Daily life application: The next time you get upset about something or have strong feelings that you want to express, do the previous drawing and writing activity. If the feelings are really strong, you may need bigger paper to draw on. Try using crayons and draw on an old newspaper or plain newsprint. Do the reflective writing from step 3 in your journal. This is a great stress-buster, as it lets you safely release pent-up emotions.

<hr />

Another way to experience your Inner Child is to actually draw a picture of it and have a written dialogue.

Child Chat

Materials: Journal and felt pens or crayons

Purpose: To learn the language of the child (visual expression); to give voice to the Inner Child's feelings and needs in words

Activity:
1. With your *nondominant* hand, let your Inner Child draw a picture of itself. Don't worry about aesthetic merit or artistic ability. Be a little kid again. Let your Inner Child do the drawing. If you find yourself being critical of the drawing, simply be aware of that fact and continue drawing anyway.
2. Using *both hands,* have a written dialogue with your Inner Child. Starting with your *dominant* hand, ask your Inner Child to tell you about itself—its name, age, how it feels, its likes and dislikes, what it needs from you. Write the answers to these questions with your *nondominant* hand.

Note: This dialogue can be done repeatedly. The answers will change each time you do it. Sometimes the Inner Child's name is different, or its age may change: one day it's three years old, another day it's nine, sometimes it's a teenager. Sometimes its gender may change, too. These variations in response are all normal and natural. Don't try to change them. It may seem that there are many Inner Children. They are just different aspects of the same part of your being. Simply accept whatever answers your Inner Child gives you, no matter how irrational or off-the-wall. Remember, the Inner Child self is not about logic and reason; it's about feelings and intuition.

MEET YOUR INNER PARENTS

The role of the Inner Parents is the same as that of parents in the outer world. The job of the Inner Parents is to care for and protect the Inner Child. How your Inner Parents treat your Inner Child is shaped by how your parents or guardians treated you as you were growing up. If they were unconditionally loving and supportive, then you probably treat your Inner Child in much the same way. If you were raised with criticism, violence, or neglect, then you are likely to relate in a similar way to your Inner Child. We learn what we see and hear.

There are three distinct facets to the Inner Parent. One of them is the *Nurturing Parent*. As the name implies, this parent specializes in nurturance. Another parent is the *Protective Parent*. This one makes things safe for the Inner Child by setting limits and boundaries on the outer world. The Protective Parent also sets limits and boundaries on the Inner Child's behavior so that we do not indulge in childish behavior. The third parent is the *Critical Parent,* who excels in negative self-talk. It plays back to us some variation of the criticism we received while growing up. The Critical Parent voice is dedicated to nagging, judging, and faultfinding.

THE NURTURING PARENT WITHIN

The Nurturing Parent's job is to listen to your Inner Child's feelings and needs and do something about them. A healthy Nurturing Parent within has a great capacity for empathy and compassion, is a good listener, values feelings and intuition and matters of the soul. If your Inner Child is physically tired and needs rest, it is your healthy Nurturing Parent who sees to it that you get a nap, go to bed earlier, or get enough sleep at night. If your job is robbing your Inner Child of its need to be creative and joyful, your Nurturing Parent will want to do something about it. If you are getting sick and tired of taking

care of everyone else and ignoring your own needs, your healthy
Nurturing Parent will heed the signs and stop to listen to your
Inner Child. The effective Nurturing Parent will always move
toward healthy decisions and actions.

In the "Child Chat" exercise earlier in the chapter, it was
your Nurturing Parent who could listen lovingly to your Inner
Child and feel empathy when unmet needs were expressed. The
Nurturing Parent is concerned with your well-being and
growth. It feeds the child self in every way: physically, emotionally, mentally, and spiritually.

Now, many people have told me they simply don't have a
Nurturing Parent within. "When you say 'Nurturing Parent,' I
draw a blank," some of them tell me. "My parents were drunk
all the time. They were incapable of nurturing me." Others say,
"I don't know what a Nurturing Parent looks like. I felt abandoned growing up. My parents worked all the time. We raised
ourselves (or were raised by a succession of baby-sitters). What
does a caring parent act like? I'd like to know." They may have
had overly perfectionistic parents. "When I think of the word
parent, all I can remember is criticism and impossible standards.
My parents didn't even like kids. They expected me to be a
grown-up, especially if I cried or was vulnerable in any way."

The paradox is that when I ask these adults what they do for
a living, they often tell me they are in the helping professions:
doctors, nurses, therapists, teachers, and so on. Or they are
servers in restaurants or managers of hotels or in some way are
responsible for directly taking care of the needs of others. "Then
you have to be sensitive to the needs of the people you serve. Is
that right?" I ask them.

"You bet I do," they answer. "If I want to keep working and
if I want to do a good job, I have to find out what my client [or
patient or customer] needs and be sure they get it." When I
mirror back to them that they are nurturing others all the time,
they usually agree. "Sure, I guess you'd say I'm a professional
nurturer. It's what I'm paid to do." These people are often very
conscientious parents as well, who put a lot of time and effort
into meeting their children's needs. "My kids come first," they
frequently say. But sometimes they go overboard and do too

much for their kids. "Then you do have a Nurturing Parent in there," I observe. "It's just that all the nurturing is going out, and none is being kept for yourself." At this point, a lightbulb goes on in their heads.

You might wonder why someone who had no nurturing in childhood would be so good at nurturing others in adulthood. Usually it is because in childhood, they had to take on adult roles and be caretakers to their parents, who couldn't assume adult responsibility. For instance, many adult children of alcoholics and addicts tell me they had to cook, clean, and do all the domestic chores at a very early age because their parents were incapable of managing their household or their lives. In other words, the roles were reversed. They were in the parent role to their own parents. We call this the parentified child.

Parentified children learn caretaking behavior, but not necessarily healthy nurturing. It may *look* like nurturance, but it's really not. Underneath the enforced, premature caretaking of a parent, there are usually deep feelings of resentment, emptiness, abandonment, and low self-esteem. "There must be something wrong with me if my parents won't or can't take care of me like other kids' parents do or like the parents in TV sitcoms do."

In becoming a parent, it is extremely important that you recognize the difference between caretaking behavior and real, honest-to-goodness nurturing. It is essential that you know how to nurture yourself. If you don't, you can't really nurture your child. You can't give from an empty cup. Don't fall into the trap of going through the motions of caretaking your family while missing the deeper emotional and spiritual needs that you all have for true nurturance. In recalling her childhood, one woman described the effects of being raised without nurturance:

> My mother was a full-time supermom of her generation. She pushed herself to be perfect, to keep an immaculate house (you could eat off the floors), be a great cook and seamstress, chauffeur, and all the rest of it. She never rested. We wanted for nothing—physically. Emotionally, it was a different story. I always felt like an intruder in "her house." Neatness, cleanliness, punctuality, and good ap-

pearances were everything. She demanded the same perfection from us that she expected in herself. There was no room for mistakes, for feelings, for spontaneity. It was not a child-friendly environment. There wasn't much emotional nourishment there.

On top of all this, Mom always complained about how much she did for us kids. But we never asked her to sacrifice herself for us. Of course, she never told us what her needs were. I don't think she knew. Maybe as a mother, she thought she wasn't supposed to have any needs. I realize now that I've been very hard on myself—the way my mother was on herself (and me)—because I thought that's what parents were supposed to do. I'm having to learn to listen to my feelings, my body, my vulnerability, and my real wishes. I don't want to be a martyr mother. It's really hard on the kids. I should know. I was raised by one.

How to Develop a Nurturing Parent Within

We learn to be an effective Nurturing Parent to our Inner Child from seeing role models of nurturing as we grow up. It might be a parent or relative; it might be a neighbor, teacher, or friend of the family. Some adults whose parents weren't very nurturing tell me they found role models for the Nurturing Parent in books or movies, or in history. Helen Keller's teacher, Annie Sullivan, was the model of a Nurturing Parent for Sharon, a young handicapped woman who was training to become a teacher. Sharon wrote journal dialogues with Miss Sullivan and received much comfort and guidance. In my own life, Maria Montessori was a strong professional role model for me about how to respect and nourish the child-spirit in the classroom.

A Word of Caution: If you experienced abuse or trauma in childhood, these exercises in self-reparenting may bring up a lot of feelings from the past. If at any time while doing these exercises you feel overwhelmed with emotions regarding your childhood, I urge you to seek professional help. This work may be too much for you to do alone. You need not attempt the work of healing your childhood in isolation. There are many well-trained and highly experienced therapists and counselors who can assist you in reclaiming the childhood that you lost. When seeking professional help, always consult with your Inner Child through journal dialogues. If you interview a professional counselor, find out how your Inner Child feels about the person. Pay close attention to the answers.

And now, let's get on with cultivating your innate ability to nurture your Inner Child. As you do this more and more, the job of nurturing your family will become much more rewarding.

Finding the Nurturing Parent

Materials: Journal and felt pens

Purpose: To reflect upon your own experiences of nurturance as you were growing up; to become aware of your own definitions of a Nurturing Parent

Activity:

1. Go back into your childhood or adolescent years. Ask yourself: Who are the people who really nurtured me as a child? As a teenager? Who provided nourishment for my body? Who cared for me when I was sick? What about my emotions? Who listened to and respected my feelings? Who comforted me and nurtured my soul? Who encouraged my talents and unique abilities? Who gave me the most loving quality of nurturance?

2. With your *nondominant* hand, write about those people who nurtured you as a child. Were there more than one? Write down the name of each one and describe specifically how each person nurtured you.

3. With your *dominant* hand, write a thank-you note to one of these nurturing people from your childhood or adolescence. Tell the person how he or she nurtured you. What did that person's caring teach you about yourself? About your worth? About how to take care of yourself?

4. With your *nondominant* hand, draw a picture of a loving

parent nurturing a little child. Perhaps the adult is holding the child in his or her arms. Maybe the child is sick or scared and the parent is providing warmth and comfort. Let your own image of a Nurturing Parent and child appear on the page.

5. Using *both hands alternately*, write a dialogue between the Nurturing Parent and the Inner Child in your picture. What does the child say? How does he or she feel? What does the child need? How does the child want the parent to take care of him or her? Let the parent ask the questions with your *dominant* hand. The Inner Child responds with the *nondominant* hand.

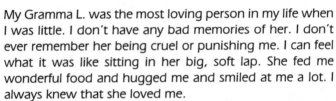

> My Gramma L. was the most loving person in my life when I was little. I don't have any bad memories of her. I don't ever remember her being cruel or punishing me. I can feel what it was like sitting in her big, soft lap. She fed me wonderful food and hugged me and smiled at me a lot. I always knew that she loved me.
>
> My Auntie N. was just like her, too, and she was the other person I remember from those early years. They both took care of me 'cause Mommy and Daddy were working during the day. Auntie N. used to take me to hear music and see art, and she even took me to her job, where they had a place for kids to paint and do art. I am still close to her today. She's such a loving and fun person.
>
> My mommy and daddy weren't around so much in those years. I don't remember my mom so much from the time before I started school, but my dad used to take me to the park sometimes to feed the ducks and go in the boats on the lake. I liked that.

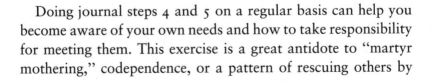

Doing journal steps 4 and 5 on a regular basis can help you become aware of your own needs and how to take responsibility for meeting them. This exercise is a great antidote to "martyr mothering," codependence, or a pattern of rescuing others by helping them avoid the consequences of their irresponsible be-havior.

There is another aspect of the Inner Parent that is essential and works hand in hand with the Nurturing Parent. It is the Protective Parent.

THE PROTECTIVE PARENT WITHIN

The Protective Parent is entrusted with the job of setting boundaries and limits so that the Inner Child does not get hurt emotionally or physically. I think of the motto "To protect and serve." The Protective Parent is a child's rights advocate, ever alert for people and situations that threaten the Inner Child's well-being. The Protective Parent also works internally to set limits on the bratty Inner Child who would take over if it could. This "Inner Brat" is the angry and defiant part of us that can throw temper tantrums in the outer world and generally behave in an infantile manner. One thinks of Arthur (played by Dudley Moore) in the movie of the same name. Another example of an Inner Brat acting out in the life of an adult is the character of Melvin (played by Jack Nicholson) in the movie *As Good as It Gets*.

Without a Protective Parent in place, it's easy for Inner Child work (as it is often called) to degenerate into indulgence of childish behavior. When this happens, either the Inner Brat or the vulnerable child takes over. Throwing temper tantrums, car-rying teddy bears around in public, or talking baby talk does *not* constitute Inner Child or Inner Family work. In fact, this aberration has gotten Inner Child work a bad name.

The Protective Parent is crucial in relationships. Without it, we can easily be taken advantage of or abused. Women who are struggling with spousal abuse are really in need of a Protective Parent within. In cases such as these, we see how the lack of a Protective Parent within the woman affects her children. If a woman cannot protect herself from her husband's violence, how can she protect her children? Clearly, she cannot. Nor can she provide her children with a good example of limit setting and boundaries. Her children grow up with no one to teach them about their own inner Protective Parent. And so the pattern is handed down from one generation to the next.

Fortunately, it is possible to develop the Protective Parent within. For self-protection is an innate human ability, and all we need are the right tools for recovering it and the willingness to use them.

The Protective Parent and the Inner Child

Materials: Journal and felt pens

Purpose: To become aware of your Protective Parent within; to find out what kind of a job your Protective Parent is doing

Activity:

1. With your *dominant* hand, draw a picture of your Protective Parent and your Inner Child. Show the parent in the act of protecting the child in some way—for example, shielding it from harm, preventing danger from befalling it, defending the child's rights.
2. Write a dialogue between your Protective Parent and your Inner Child. The parent writes with the *dominant* hand, the child with the *nondominant* hand. Using contrasting colors for this dialogue, ask the child to tell you what situations or people are threatening in your life right now. Also ask the child to describe specifically what kind of protection he or she wants in these situations.

I recommend doing this exercise on a regular basis. If you have a background of child abuse or have been abused as an adult, it's a good idea to do this journal process once a week or even more frequently.

What does this symbol of protection represent? What kinds of protection do you need?

> I need help! Help, help, help! Let me out, out, out! Don't keep me behind a wall! Let me out but don't let me go unprotected. Shield me from harm from hurtful glances and harmful criticism.
>
> Let me out, *out, out!* I want to play, not be cooped up all the time! Let me *out!* Don't censor me! I need to speak! Let me out! I'm OK, so let me play! I want to go out! Don't tell me I'm wrong! OK?

What situations or people feel threatening to you?

- Failure; mean people
- Crowded places
- Pain, physical or emotional
- New things
- Expecting great things from me

What exactly do you need me to do to protect you?

- Learn to be more self-secure.
- Tell me that it's safe for me to come out.
- Tell me that it's OK.
- Let me feel and cry.

What situations or people feel threatening to you?

> People who are mean or abusive. Situations that are out of control. When I am not protected. When there is no defense.

What exactly do you want me to do to protect you?

> To listen to me and believe me.

A Nurturing Parent is essential, as we have seen earlier, but without a Protective Parent in place, you can't take care of your Inner Child when facing overdemanding people or situations. Cultivating a strong Protective Parent within will pay dividends in those situations in which you have to assert yourself or take action on behalf of your Inner Child's needs. It is the Protective Parent within who can "just say no" to others who don't respect your wishes or needs. For this Inner Parent is impersonal, businesslike, and clear in its communication with others. This aspect

of the Inner Parent is a great ally in all business dealings, negotiations, or conflicts of any kind. The Protective Parent is not
concerned with seeking approval or whether it is popular. It
knows how to "do the right thing." It is the keeper of your real
values, knows what is important to you, communicates your
needs to others, and sticks to its guns. You cannot have a better
helpmate than the Protective Parent when it comes to setting
limits for your child (in the outer world) or for your Inner Child.

And now we move on to the third parent, the one I call the
"shadow" parent, to borrow from Jungian psychology, because
most of us are not consciously aware of exactly how this one
operates. And as with all the shadow parts of the self, it is in
our ignorance of it that we are undone by it. I'm speaking of the
Critical Parent.

THE CRITICAL PARENT WITHIN

The Critical Parent's mission in life is to judge, criticize, and
try to control the Inner Child. This parent has its roots in a
survival mechanism that all children must learn as they adapt to
a world run by adults. This Critical Parent is steeped in the
shoulds and oughts that you learned as a child. It recites them
to you constantly. Unfortunately, while reminding you of all the
duties and responsibilities you must handle or the jobs you have
shirked or failed, the Critical Parent indulges in character assas-
sination. It frequently insults you, raises impossible standards,
and generally puts you in a no-win position. You can never
please the Critical Parent. It's a perfectionist who pressures you
to always be better, different, or something other than who you
are. It says things like "You're too tall. You're too fat. You're
ugly. You're stupid." If we fail, it never stops reminding us of
the fact. When we succeed at something, it warns us that we
might fail next time or that our success wasn't big enough.

All of this is not to say that we don't need to grow and mature
and develop ourselves. We certainly do. That is the basis of all
religions, spiritual practices, and psychological methods: fulfilling our true potential by becoming more conscious and behaving with awareness. But the Critical Parent is usually out of

control and actually sabotages our growth process. It is *not* our conscience (which helps us to become more self-aware and act in accordance with our values). Rather, it is the voice of negative judgment, damaging our confidence and sense of self-worth. If unchecked, the Critical Parent can do great harm in all areas of our lives: career, health, relationships, finances.

If we think we are worthless because our Critical Parent told us so, then we will behave accordingly. We may look to others to make us feel worthwhile. Life then becomes an unending search for approval and love in all the wrong places. Parents caught in this trap are so desperate for their children to *like* them that they find it impossible to set limits and boundaries. All the child has to do is cry and this doormat parent caves in.

In self-reparenting, we unmask the Critical Parent and see it for what it is: an emperor with no clothes. The Critical Parent lives in our own heads, and it has only as much power as we give it. It is part of the human condition—factory equipment, so to speak—and we can't get rid of it. But we can find out how it operates and put it into perspective.

Curious as to the function of the Inner Critic in the overall scheme of things, I once asked my Inner Guide, "Why do we have a Critical Parent within?" It answered, "To test you. And strengthen your faith in yourself and in the divine. The Inner Critic teaches you to have resolve and determination, to be a spiritual warrior. By learning to see through its attacks, you wake up to the truth of who you really are."

In the next journal exercise, you'll have a chance to bring your Inner Critic out of the closet and find out exactly what it is saying to you every day. Don't be surprised if some of its dialogue is painfully familiar and reminiscent of your childhood. After all, your inner Critical Parent was trained by your parents or guardians as you were growing up. The themes may have changed to some extent, but the underlying message is the same. Now it's "What a hopelessly lazy slob. You didn't do your taxes," and then it was "What a hopelessly lazy slob. You didn't do your homework." Shaming and blaming and insults to your character didn't work then, and they don't work now. Such put-downs only produce defiance and keep you stuck in reactive, nonproductive behavior. So here's a way to get out from under the thumb of your Inner Critic.

The Critical Parent and the Inner Child

Materials: Journal, felt pens, and crayons

Purpose: To become aware of your Critical Parent within; to disidentify from the blaming and shaming of negative self-talk

Activity:

1. With your *dominant* hand, draw a picture of your Critical Parent scolding your Inner Child. Draw this like a cartoon or comic strip. Show both parent and child in your picture. First put word bubbles beside the Critical Parent containing some of its favorite phrases at this time in your life. Write them with your *dominant* hand. Write them in the second person just as if a parent were talking to the child. "You're a mess. Look at this house." "Boy, are you stupid. Look at all the mistakes in your work. You're hopeless."

2. Beside the Inner Child in the drawing, put word bubbles containing the child's feelings about what the Critical Parent has said. Write the feelings with your *nondominant* hand.

3. On the next page in your journal, using your *dominant* hand, write down all the put-down messages your Critical Parent whispers in your ear each day. You know, all that negative stuff you tell yourself. Be sure to put it in the second person ("You're too fat"; or "You'll never pay off all these debts. You're the worst manager of money I've ever seen"; or "Look at your hair. How can you go out in public looking like that?"; or "This house is a mess. You're the worst housekeeper in the neighborhood. How can you live like this?").

4. Reread what your Critical Parent just wrote. Let yourself

feel whatever reaction you have to what it said. On the next page in your journal, using your *nondominant* hand, let your Inner Child answer back. You have my permission to let your Inner Brat out to sass the Critical Parent back. Have fun with this.

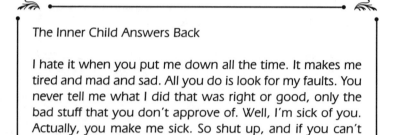

The Inner Child Answers Back

I hate it when you put me down all the time. It makes me tired and mad and sad. All you do is look for my faults. You never tell me what I did that was right or good, only the bad stuff that you don't approve of. Well, I'm sick of you. Actually, you make me sick. So shut up, and if you can't say anything nice, just stay out of my life!

Daily life application: Some people find that they have a lot of steam to let off at their Critical Parent. If you find that that's the case, you might want to write your Inner Child's response with big kindergarten crayons on pages of old newspapers. When your Critical Parent gets you down, feeling inadequate and discouraged, repeat this exercise.

During the day, be aware of the Critical Parent's voice chattering in your head. Then bring your mind back to what you were doing before the inner chatter interrupted your concentration. Let go of the Critical Parent's voice and refocus on your activity. This is a great form of meditation and an excellent technique for cleansing your mind of toxic thoughts.

Note: For an in-depth program on Inner Child and Inner Family work, you can refer to my book *Recovery of Your Inner Child* and my audiotape *The Inner Family* in *The Wisdom of Your Other Hand* (a collection of five tapes produced by Sounds True).

4

The World within Your Home

In this chapter, you'll be deepening and extending the skills you've learned so far. There will be techniques for reducing stress, for learning to nurture yourself and your family, and for getting clearer about the quality of family life you want. It's all about creating a nurturing attitude and atmosphere in your home.

We live in a time and a society that offers us many blessings. We enjoy freedoms and opportunities that humans have never had before: democracy, freedom of speech, education for all, access to tools, and huge amounts of information. The *global village* (a term coined by Marshall McLuhan in the 1960s) has now become a reality. Yet everything comes with a price. Along with our high standard of living, extended life expectancy, and amazing technological advances, we have created a world that has become dizzyingly complex and stressful for adults and children alike.

Television programming reflects the fact that we live in a violent society. Children and young people are killed or maimed in gang-related warfare or by individuals run amok. It happens in the inner cities and suburbs and rural areas as well. Sometimes these outbursts even occur in schools and classrooms, as in the tragic massacre at Columbine High in Littleton, Colorado, which took place as I was writing this book. One wonders: Is there no safe place for children? When I was growing up in Los Angeles, we played on the street, walked and rode our bikes all over the place, and never feared for our safety. The world was a much friendlier place then. Today I wonder how many children have the kind of freedom of movement we had. Must they travel through virtual reality on their computer screens instead of exploring the neighborhood as we once did? And we're finding that even the Internet poses threats to children. Where is it safe for them?

In the context of such a world, you might ask: What's a parent to do? How do I create safety for myself and my child? Some parents choose to work in careers or jobs that make the world a better place to live. I certainly felt that way about my Head Start work. Others get actively involved in their community, helping to create more child-friendly neighborhoods and environments. If you can, by all means work to change the outer world for the better. But don't forget to start at home.

IT ALL BEGINS AT HOME

You may have little control over what's going on in that big world around you, but there is one place where you are in charge: your home. If you want to create a safe, less stressful atmosphere in which to raise your child, you can start right where you are. Start with yourself—with how you manage time and stress, how you take care of your body and mind, and how you relate to the environment of your home. In this chapter, you will find techniques for dealing with these issues.

Let's begin by looking at what prevents us from relaxing and enjoying ourselves and our children. One of the greatest causes of stress for parents today is that they are all trying to *do* so much: work; commute long distances; maintain households; have a social life; improve their education; keep physically, psychologically, and spiritually fit; and—oh, yes—raise a family, too. There are school plays to attend and sports events and science fairs and PTA meetings and teacher conferences and piano lessons and doctors' appointments and . . . and . . . and . . . You fill in the blanks. I run out of breath when I see what many parents are doing these days. And I get downright exhausted when I see the schedules of some children. After a full school day, there are after-school tutorials; private lessons in music, dance, or martial arts; homework; and household chores. I wonder what happens to spontaneous play or just relaxing or "hanging out" with the family (and I don't mean vegetating for hours in front of the television set).

I first began observing this pattern some years ago among therapy clients. It seemed as if there were an epidemic going on. I came to identify it as an addiction to "doing too much" (or what Marian Woodman calls the addiction to perfection). This addiction had almost killed me, so I had firsthand experience with its symptoms. Many of my clients suffering with this malady were women with young children or teenagers. They were struggling with burnout and were being treated for stress-related disorders and autoimmune diseases, such as chronic fatigue syndrome and Epstein-Barr virus. I will share with you what I learned about healing this condition of "doing too much." Incidentally, Jungian analyst and storyteller Clarissa Pinkola Estes writes eloquently about this deep dis-ease of the soul in her book *Women Who Run with the Wolves*. I recommend it.

'TIS A GIFT TO BE SIMPLE

To counteract the pattern of "doing too much" and carrying more responsibility than is healthy, start by simplifying your life. Yes, that's right. Get back to basics and down to the essentials. This begins with clarifying your values (the work you did in Chapter 2) and setting priorities regarding time and energy output. Simplifying your life means letting go of the things that clutter up your life and drain your energy. That includes pent-up emotions, worries, toxic people and situations, as well as "stuff" and activities that you don't really need. The dialogues with your Inner Child from Chapter 3 will help tremendously in this regard.

Dropping unrealistic and perfectionistic expectations of yourself and your child is another good stress reduction strategy. You began this process in Chapter 3 when you learned how to deal with your Critical Parent and refused to be controlled by its impossible demands. Focusing on what you want instead of what you don't want will also take you toward your goals and counteract feelings of frustration and dissatisfaction. (You did that in Chapter 2 when you inventoried your values and reflected on your own style of parenting.)

So let's continue with more exercises, this time with a focus on simplifying your life. This activity deals with time—how we use it, how we lose it, and how we can take charge of it.

The Time Pie

Materials: Journal and felt pens or crayons

Purpose: To simplify your life; to manage time according to your priorities

Activity:
1. Use two pages side by side in your journal. On the left-hand page, draw a large circle. Title this page "Before."
2. Divide this circle into pie-shaped pieces that represent the activities of a typical week in your life. The size of each "slice" will represent the amount of time you devote to that activity. Categories should include such things as eating, sleeping, shopping, cooking, cleaning, household maintenance, personal grooming, working a job, time with family and friends, hobbies, and so forth. With your *dominant* hand, draw a symbol for that particular activity inside each pie segment and write in a label (from the categories suggested above).
3. Look over this "time pie" that you just created. Does it represent your real values and priorities? Is there any activity you'd like to change, expand, reduce, or drop altogether? Is there anything missing from your time pie?

4. On the right-hand page of your journal, using your *non-dominant* hand, label the page "After." On this page, draw in a new circle and pie shapes showing how you'd *like* to manage your time. What activities are essential? Which are important to you? Which do you want to make more time for? Which would you like to make less time for? Are any of these activities expendable?

Daily life application: Sit down with your calendar or daily planner book and incorporate the changes shown in your second time pie. Focus on simplifying your schedule. Throughout the day, keep asking yourself: Is this activity really necessary? If not, can I drop it? Or delegate it to someone else? Try it out for a week and see how things go. This may take awhile, but it's worth the time required to gain control of your time and your life.

THE SIMPLE LIFE

Another way to get down to the essentials is to get rid of things that you no longer need. If you aren't using it, chances are it's time to toss it or pass it on to someone who will use it. There's a deep feeling of freedom that comes from doing this process. It clears the space and reminds you that you are not owned by your possessions. Obviously, if something has deep sentimental value for you, keep it. You'll know the difference.

Cleaning House

Materials: Old cardboard boxes, shopping bags, or other containers

Purpose: To rid yourself of what you don't need; to lighten your load

Activity:

1. Do an inventory of your possessions and ask yourself whether you really need them all. You don't have to write

TIME PIE
BEFORE

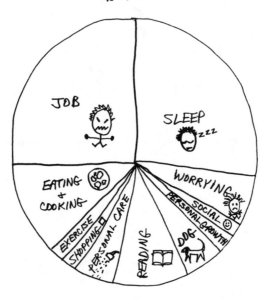

TIME PIE
AFTER

this down. Just go from room to room and look over all the "stuff" you've accumulated. Go through your wardrobe, dresser drawers, closets, kitchen cabinets, and so forth. Are you using the items there? Do you really need this old sweater that you haven't worn in three years? What about that vase you won in a raffle? Do you use it, or are you hanging onto it because it was free? Be really honest with yourself.

2. Put the "don't need" items into three piles: Pile 1 is for the Goodwill or Salvation Army. Pile 2 is to be given away to people you know who can use or appreciate the items. Pile 3 is for the trash. If you or a friend is in the custom of holding garage sales, pile 1 could be a garage sale pile. But be ruthlessly honest about this one. Don't just transfer this pile to the garage or a closet and let it sit there for months. Remember, the idea is to de-clutter your house, to clear your home of everything you don't need. Period.

3. Walk through your home and ask yourself honestly: Is this house child-friendly? Is there furniture that is comfortable for children? Are there places where they can be themselves? Engage comfortably in activities that they enjoy? Is there furniture and equipment that is age-appropriate?

FEELINGS AND STRESS

A great deal of stress is associated with emotional reactions we have toward problem situations. In trying to cope with difficult people or find solutions to daily problems, we often build up incredible amounts of unexpressed feelings. This causes tension in our bodies. If we think that showing disappointment or frustration or anger or sadness is not "the adult thing to do," we may bury our emotions. The trouble with this is that emotions don't go away. They just hang out in the body and the mind. Practitioners of body-oriented therapies—such as therapeutic massage, Rolfing, and Myofascial Release work—say that the body stores unacknowledged feelings as if it were a closet. Pent-up emotions wreak havoc with our health and psychological well-being. A person who is a "pain in the neck" can easily cause us to have one. Any situation we refer to as "a headache" can cause that, too. These commonly used phrases didn't get into our vocabulary for nothing. I've seen clients clear up many a physical ache or pain when they cleared up a relationship, either by leaving it or by confronting the person. It's happened in my own life many, many times.

This is especially important for parents. On top of the awesome responsibility of raising a child, you simply can't afford to stuff stress into your body or mind in the form of unexpressed feelings. Better to let off some steam in a safe way than to have it misfire and get directed at your child or other loved ones. Don't use your family for target practice. We all do it, but we don't have to. If you're angry at your boss, it's OK to admit it to your family. Be honest about it. But don't get back at the boss by being mean to your child. There's nothing to gain and everything to lose.

Your children need to know that you have the same kind of feelings they do. I learned this from my daughter Aleta in one of the biggest compliments she ever paid me. She was about eight years old; our lives were in crisis because of a recent divorce and illness. I went to my room and sat down and just started sobbing. She heard me and came in and sat down next to me on the edge of the bed. I tried to wipe my tears, thinking that I shouldn't upset her with my sadness. "It's OK to cry, Mom. That's what I love about you. When you're sad, you're *really* sad. And when you're happy, you're *really* happy. I always know where you stand." It was one of those great parent-child moments that one never forgets.

Once More with Feeling

Materials: Journal and felt pens; optional: large paper and crayons

Purpose: To release pent-up emotions; to acknowledge our true feelings in the face of problem situations

Activity:

1. Think about a current situation or a person who is a problem for you. With your *dominant* hand, write down in your journal all the things that are troubling you in relation to this situation or person.

2. With your *nondominant* hand, on the next journal page, draw a picture of the problem: a symbol, abstract shapes and colors, or a scene portraying the troubling situation.

3. Still using your *nondominant* hand, draw an outline of a person. This is your body. Then color in the areas where you carry your tension, stress, and emotions about this situation.

4. With your *nondominant* hand, on another page, draw just the feelings that you colored in on your body outline. If more than one body part is affected, take them one at a time. Imagine that you are releasing these emotions from your body out onto the paper. Use any form of expression you like: scribbling, doodling, making shapes and colors. Use colors that express the feelings. Then write the feeling words in and around your drawing.

    Note: If the feelings are very strong, you might want to draw them out on a larger piece of art paper or newsprint using crayons and felt pens.

5. Using *both hands alternately,* write a dialogue between yourself and the problem person or situation. Write your part with the *dominant* hand and the part of the problem person or situation with your *nondominant* hand.

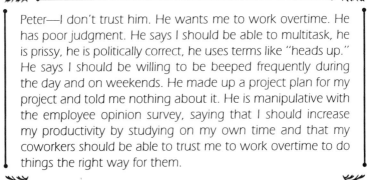

Peter—I don't trust him. He wants me to work overtime. He has poor judgment. He says I should be able to multitask, he is prissy, he is politically correct, he uses terms like "heads up." He says I should be willing to be beeped frequently during the day and on weekends. He made up a project plan for my project and told me nothing about it. He is manipulative with the employee opinion survey, saying that I should increase my productivity by studying on my own time and that my coworkers should be able to trust me to work overtime to do things the right way for them.

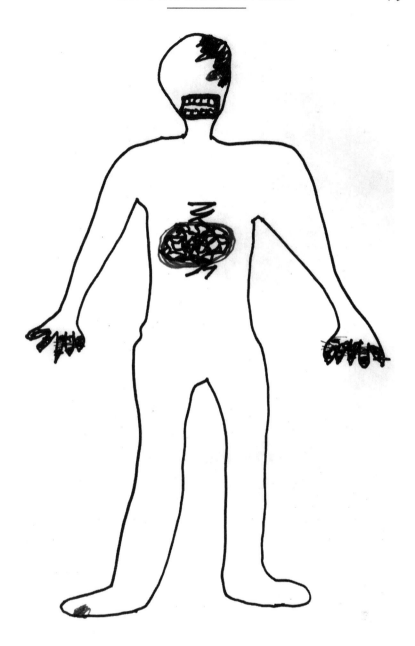

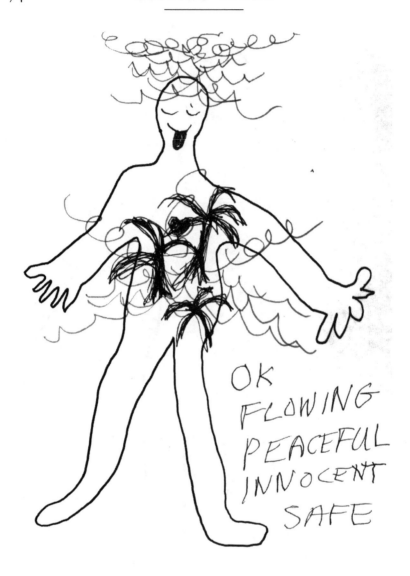

OK
FLOWING
PEACEFUL
INNOCENT
SAFE

JOURNALING STRESS AWAY

There is a power in silence and in solitude that our results-oriented civilization has lost sight of. For that reason, people are starved for peace and quiet. Books and tapes on meditation are selling better than ever. Workshops on the subject are filled. Journaling has come into the mainstream as a topic for authors and teachers all over the country. My first book, *The Creative*

Journal, has been out since 1980, yet in the last few years, it has sold better than ever. More and more people find that they want to sit quietly and reflect on their lives. They want to get off the treadmill of incessant activity and reassess who they are, what they want, and where they're going.

One of the greatest gifts you can give yourself as a parent is some quiet time with yourself. I know this isn't easy to come by, especially if you work and if you have more than one child. But it is possible—if you make it a priority and build it into your life. And as your child grows, you might introduce him or her to *The Creative Journal for Children* and inaugurate "family journal time" so that self-reflection becomes a customary practice. I know of many families who do this.

One young man, Steven, told me that journaling time had brought him and his wife and stepson much closer together. Steven and his wife, Cynthia, were both veteran journal-keepers before they met. After they married, they decided to reserve quiet time every evening for journaling, and they gave Cynthia's son, Todd, his own journal. In addition to these daily sessions, they use their journals to sort through difficult issues when they come up. As Steven explained:

> The insights we gain help us communicate more clearly with each other. For myself, knowing how I feel about something instead of blaming Todd or Cynthia or trying to change them has made all the difference in the world. If I can get in touch with what I want and need, things seem to clear up pretty quickly. And Todd is amazing now. In his journal, he wrote that he used to be afraid I'd take Cynthia away from him. After he shared that, the whining and manipulating he used to do just stopped, and at age nine, he can tell us how he feels and what he really needs.

If you've been doing the journal exercises in the previous chapter, you probably know what a calming effect journaling has. I know of very few practices—besides meditation, prayer, and expressive arts—that relieve stress as quickly, inexpensively, and effectively as journaling. It is my hope by the time you've completed the work in this book, journaling will become a regular practice. As one friend said, "If you've got to have an addiction, journaling is a darned good one." I agree.

SPIRITUALITY AND STRESS

In conjunction with journaling, two other great stress-busters are prayer and meditation. Prayer has been described as "talking to God," and meditation has been defined as "God talking to you." Journaling is a wonderful way to cultivate either practice.

Writing your own prayers is a very special journal exercise. It brings prayer to life and personalizes it. You can pray to God, Mother Nature, your favorite saint, your Higher Power, Universal Mind, or use whatever name you like for the Creator. Entering the silent temple of your heart and allowing your own prayer to find a voice is one of the most strengthening and calming things you can do.

My Prayer

Materials: Journal and felt pens

Purpose: To cultivate the practice of prayer; to create your own prayers

Activity:
1. Take a few minutes to contemplate all the blessings you enjoy in your life. With your *dominant* hand, write a prayer of thanksgiving.
2. Reflect upon the area(s) of your life that need healing. With your *nondominant* hand, write a prayer in which you ask for help and for healing.

Prayer of Thanksgiving
I humbly come before you, my heavenly father, with praise and thanksgiving, for I know it is you who keeps me in a healthy and safe environment. Thank you for giving me my children and allowing us to be happy together again. For you know what is best for us.

The Past Is the Past
The past is the past. I choose to leave it there. I know old wounds die hard. I give all this pain and misery to you, for I can no longer bear it. As I let go, I will not take it back. Thank you for loving me until I can love myself.

SITTING STILL

Another great antidote to stress is meditation. Just sitting quietly and entering the silence within can do wonders for a harassed and tired parent. Research by Herbert Benson at Harvard and by Elmer and Alyce Green at the Meninger Clinic (to cite only two examples) has shown that meditation has tremendous benefits, not only for the body but for the mind as well. Meditation has been shown to lower high blood pressure, calm the nervous system, alleviate pain, increase energy levels, and help relieve insomnia.

I recommend meditating on a regular basis. I know, I know. You're wondering, Where am I going to find the time for all this? If all you have is five minutes, that's a great place to start. It doesn't take long to receive the benefits from this simple practice. It is in the silence of meditation that our intuition and our creative self really have a chance to speak to us. It is that "still, small voice within" that speaks to us in meditation. It is the source of our inner wisdom and of love.

Peace and Quiet

Materials: Journal and felt pens

Purpose: To experience the inner silence of meditation; to
              clear the mind for listening to the heart

Activity:

1. Find a quiet place where you can be alone for a few moments. A place in nature works well for this, such as a park or beach. Or perhaps you prefer a quiet room where you can feel at home with yourself. Sit down in a comfortable position and simply focus on your breathing. Observe the breath coming in and out. Don't try to change anything. Just be aware of your breathing and the rhythm of inhaling and exhaling. After doing this a few times, allow any tension in your body to go out with the exhale. Let yourself get rid of what you don't need each time you exhale.

2. While continuing to feel the rhythm of your breathing, quietly begin to be aware of other sensory input: smells, sights, sounds, textures, the weather, and so on.

3. Now close your eyes and observe any thoughts that come to mind. Do the thoughts take you out of the present moment? Away from your body and senses? Are you thinking about the past or the future? Observe these thoughts. Imagine that your mind is a clear blue sky. When the thoughts come up, see them as clouds passing through the sky. Then let them go. If more thoughts come up, continue observing them, allow them to come and go. Don't get attached to any particular thought or get involved in it. For example, "I should have had my green dress dry-cleaned for the meeting on Friday. Maybe I need some other things cleaned. I'd better . . ." Ah, another thought that has nothing to do with the present moment. Let it go.

4. In your journal, with your *nondominant* hand, jot down any observations or insights you had as a result of meditating.

THE PEOPLE IN YOUR LIFE

In cultures where families are large and connected by a huge network of relatives, there exists a built-in support system for young people who are raising children. The fact is that the concept of the nuclear family (two parents and their children living in their own dwelling) is a very recent invention. In modern industrialized nations, the bloodline extended family is becoming extinct. Our rate of mobility is increasing; people no longer are born, live, and die in the same place; and it is expected that adults who are raising children of their own will have their own place to live.

The nuclear family puts a great burden on parents, and it is no surprise that this new family configuration has spawned a high divorce rate. This, in turn, puts an even greater burden on single parents, who must carry all or most of the responsibility for child rearing on their own shoulders. What is the solution to this dilemma of isolation and backbreaking responsibility that the nuclear family imposes? One answer is the extended-family-by-choice. However, before we begin to build a supportive network of friends, neighbors, professionals, and so forth, it's important to do some "spring cleaning" again.

People Inventory

A major stress factor in our lives is toxic people. What defines a toxic person? A toxic person is someone who drains your energy, makes you feel inadequate, criticizes you, pressures you, or consistently shows that he or she doesn't accept you as you are. This is a very personal judgment call. A person who is toxic for you may not be toxic for someone else. Sometimes blood relatives or in-laws are toxic for us because they think the familial bond gives them the right to control our lives. Or perhaps there is an active addict or deadbeat in the family who pressures you to rescue him or her and you feel guilty if you let such a relative down.

It's important to keep in mind that people who consistently engage in behavior that is toxic for you can't get away with it without your permission. Eleanor Roosevelt said it best: "Nobody can do anything to me that I'm not already doing to myself." So the work you've done in the previous chapters can help you sort out what it is you're doing to yourself that others are only mirroring. Do you still let your Critical Parent run your life? Then you'll let a person who behaves like a Critical Parent hold a lot of power over you. As you deal with inner criticism and negative self-talk, your tolerance for putting up with critical people will gradually disappear.

A good way to find out who is toxic for you is to review the exercise in Chapter 3 titled "The Protective Parent and the Inner Child." Another way is to do the following journal activity.

Energy Drains

Materials: Journal and felt pens

Purpose: To identify toxic people; to reflect upon what to do about toxic people and relationships

Activity:

1. With your *nondominant* hand, make a list of all the people who drain your energy or with whom you cannot be your real self. Under each name, jot down how you feel when you are around this person or when you even think about him or her.

2. Go back over your list and focus on each person one at a time. Is there any way you might change this relationship? Is there anything you can do to improve communication with this person? Do you feel that it is impossible for things to change? With your *dominant* hand, write any ideas that come to mind.

3. What action do you want to take about each of these relationships? Is it best or possible for you to limit time with this person? Did you get any ideas about how you might clear up the problem? Would it be healthier for you to drop this person from your life? Write down your thoughts, using your *dominant* hand.

4. If you have to be around a person who is toxic for you— for instance, at your job—do some written dialogues with *both hands* about the specific situation that is bothering

you. Write your own voice out with your *dominant* hand, and write the other person's voice with your *nondominant* hand.

Daily life application: When you are with other people, make a point of observing whether your energy is boosted or drained by being in their presence. Do you feel tension in any particular parts of your body? Afterward reflect on how much time you want to spend around that person or whether you want that person in your life at all. As you become clearer about your own worth and how you use your time, you'll become more thoughtful about the people with whom you surround yourself and your child.

Energy Drains

1. Barbara: *I have to watch my words—walk on eggshells!*
2. Hank and Lynn: *Don't let them know the real me.*
3. Linda: *Long conversations—on and on. I hear all her fear and sadness.*
4. People at O.A. meetings: *Same old shit!*

With Barbara, *I am aware that I must protect myself, and until she reaches further to me (if ever), I can and will do what I have to.*

With Hank and Lynn, *I am seeing them less and less because the relationship isn't very real. Oh, well, now that we don't have to please our mother, we don't have to "act" like brother and sister anymore, do we?*

O.A. meetings: *Try other meetings, and if I still* feel this way, *listen to myself and drop it. But replace it with more exercise!!*

YOUR EXTENDED-FAMILY-BY-CHOICE

Building a team of nurturing and mutually supportive people is one of the greatest gifts you can give to yourself and your family. In good times and bad, your freely chosen support team will function the way extended families have in all cultures. They'll be there to help, empathize, celebrate your victories, and cheer you on when you feel discouraged. A strong support system is one of the best stress preventions that I know. Without genuine support from others, we feel lonely and isolated, and family responsibilities become burdensome beyond belief. Don't be a martyr. Reach out and ask for help. Be prepared to give it, too. For support must be a two-way street or your team will fall apart. The next exercise is intended to help you identify where you receive your support and also where you need more.

My Support Team

Materials: Journal and felt pens

Purpose: To make an inventory of your existing support system; to identify the areas where you need more support

Activity:

1. With your *nondominant* hand, draw a small symbol representing yourself in the center of your journal page. Draw lines radiating out from your center picture with balloons attached to them. In each balloon, write the name of a person or group who provides you with support. These are people who are really there for you when you need them, providing assistance, understanding, or any other resources. Include all categories of helping persons: relatives, loved ones, friends, neighbors, coworkers, professionals (health care practitioners, lawyer, and so forth), teachers, mentors, and so on. Label your picture "My Support Team."

2. Look at your support system diagram. Can you think of any areas of your life in which you need support but are not getting it at the present time? On the next page in your journal, create another diagram like the one you just

drew, still using your nondominant hand. This time make bubbles for the areas where you need help. Next to each bubble, write the name of that area. If someone comes to mind who can support you in any of these areas, write his or her name (or a group name) inside the corresponding bubble. Label this "Need Support."

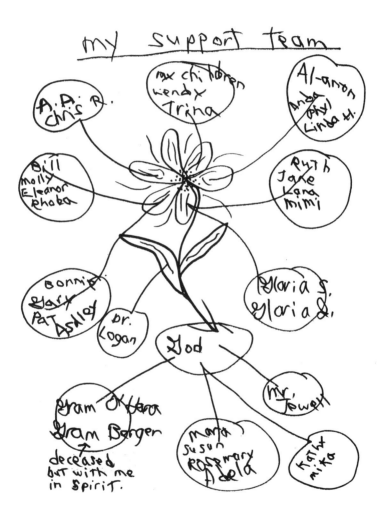

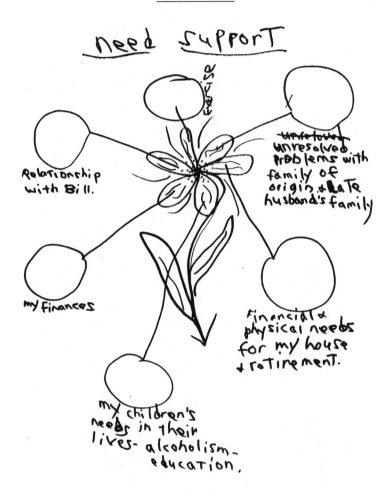

need support

exercise

Relationship with Bill.

unresolved problems with family of origin & late husband's family

my finances

financial & physical needs for my house & retirement.

my children's needs in their lives - alcoholism - education.

Daily life application: Set about to find and activate support in the areas you identified in the last diagram. Put the words "Get help for . . ." on specific days in your calendar if you think you'll forget to follow through on this.

CARING FOR YOURSELF, CARING FOR YOUR FAMILY

Taking good care of yourself and your home environment is one of the greatest ways to care for your family. If you are healthy, growing, and feel good about yourself, your family can't help but feel it in the atmosphere. In doing, doing, doing for our kids, we cannot neglect our own needs. When we do, trouble is in store. Since we received no training for healthy self-nurturing in school, this is a skill we have to learn as adults. And it isn't always easy. We may be told we're being selfish, we may have to "just say no" to others, we may feel guilty. It takes courage to do the right thing. But it will pay off in the long run. And self-care is really the best way there is to prevent stress and create a truly nourishing environment for your child.

Caring for Myself

Materials: Journal and felt pens; collage materials

Purpose: To identify people, places, things, and activities that nurture you; to expand your repertoire of nurturing elements in your life

Activity:

1. Using a double-page spread in your journal, create four columns by dividing each page in two with a vertical line from top to bottom. Label each column at the top. Column 1 is headed "Nurturing People," column 2 is "Nurturing Places," column 3 is "Nurturing Things," and column 4 is "Nurturing Activities." With your *dominant* hand, fill in the columns, writing down the ways that you have found to nurture yourself in these areas. If you run out of space, continue on another page.

2. In your journal, with your *dominant* hand, make your own list of new ways to nurture yourself. (See the list of suggestions in the accompanying box, but really be creative and invent your own.)

3. With your collage materials, create a picture titled "Taking Care of Myself."

4. Make another collage titled "A Nurturing Home." Picture the kind of nurturing elements you want in your home and in your daily life.

Resources: *The Picture of Health: Healing Your Life with Art; The Well-Being Journal.*

Caring for Myself

Nurturing People	Nurturing Places	Nurturing Things	Nurturing Activities
Mara	University of	Ocean	Watching sunsets
Maria K.	Judaism	Music (not rock)	at ocean
Judy at U.J.	Synagogue	My bed, quilt, and	Going to concerts
Betty at U.J.	My home	pillows	Cuddled up on
Jake	Florence's house	Looking at my art	couch reading
Maure	in N.Y.	at home	Watching
(sometimes)	Visit to ocean	Some clothes I	meaningful
Annette	Beautiful gardens	love and keep	movies
Florence	Mountain areas	for years	Cooking
Carole			Putting my arms
Hilary			around myself
Stefanie			Bubble bath
Ruby through			Dancing around
Maure			naked

Ways to Take Care of Myself

Go out in nature; enjoy smells, sounds, textures, and sights.
Gaze at the moon and stars.
Watch a sunset or sunrise.
Walk in the rain or snow.
Take a class or workshop.
Attend an interesting lecture.
Browse in a bookshop, hardware store, art supply store.
Call someone I haven't talked to in a long time.
Have afternoon tea with a friend.
Take a nap in the daytime.
Look at the clouds and see how many pictures I find there.
Visit an art museum or a gallery.
Play in a playground (with or without kids there).
Have breakfast in bed.
Walk in a park, hike up a hill or mountain, stroll on a beach.
Go to a concert or club to listen to my favorite music.
Make a picture and put it on the refrigerator.
Get a massage, have a facial, get my hair done.
Feel my feelings.
Buy myself a bouquet of flowers.
Do something good for Mother Nature.
Write a love letter to my Inner Child and mail it to myself.
Dance around the living room to my favorite music.
Play a musical instrument, write a poem, paint a picture.
Take a hot bath with bubbles, bath oils, and a rubber ducky.
Send a love letter to a friend or loved one.
Drive to the country or beach.
Slow down, breathe more deeply, and smell the roses.
Gaze out the window, any window.
Hug someone.
Take an invigorating walk.
Dig in a garden, plant a flower.
Listen to music with my eyes closed and do nothing else.
Have dinner by candlelight.
Watch my favorite funny movie on video.
Make an "achievement award" for myself for a difficult job well done.
Go barefoot.
Meditate, contemplate, pray.
Draw and write in my journal.
Ask for someone to help me with a difficult problem.
Pet a cat, hug a dog, appreciate an animal.
Laugh, sing, tell a joke.
Curl up with a good book.
Let myself cry.
Be spontaneous, follow a hunch.
Help a family member or friend, volunteer for a good cause.
Make space for alone time every day.
Thank God for all my blessings and lessons.

PART TWO

Welcoming a Child into Your Life

Pregnancy, Birth, and Adoption
Stepparenting and Blending Families

5

When You're Expecting

This chapter will guide you in the journey of pregnancy. Although it is intended primarily for the pregnant woman, there are journal exercises here that will benefit anyone who is welcoming a child into his or her life. This is true whether the child is coming through adoption or a partner who already has one or more children. So I recommend that you read this chapter, even if your doorway into parenting does not include pregnancy and biological birth.

As a journey, pregnancy has a finite time and character all its own. Yet in another sense, it is the beginning of a journey that has no end. For once you have experienced pregnancy, you are changed forever. The immense impact it has on your life is impossible to predict. This is as true for women who have miscarried or aborted a pregnancy as it is for those who go full term. Later in this chapter, there will be some journal work for dealing with emotions associated with infertility, difficult pregnancies, miscarriages, abortions, or infant deaths. In healing the past, it will be easier to accept the present and move into the future as a welcoming parent.

Like all journeys, pregnancy has its ups and downs, its joyful moments and its difficult ones. You will take a look at your attitudes and expectations about what pregnancy holds in store and partner, or bond, with your baby using some of the imagery and dialogue techniques you've already been introduced to. This chapter also includes practical techniques for dealing with health issues. Whether you are having a normal, healthy pregnancy or a difficult one, these methods of body/mind awareness will help you become more sensitive to the incredible changes that are taking place in your body and your emotions. Hopefully, these journal reflections will guide you in taking the best possible care of yourself and in experiencing both mental and physical well-being as you take the first steps into parenting.

ENTERING PARENTHOOD

Upon being told I was pregnant with my first child, I instinctively started having mental conversations with the soul who had chosen to enter this world through my body. I use the term *chosen* because that is truly how I felt. Being able to carry a living being within me felt like such a great honor. It was, and still is, a mystery as well. And like all mysteries, pregnancy took me to places I'd never dreamed possible, physically, emotionally, mentally, and spiritually. In looking back on that time, it is clear that the seeds of much of the professional work I am doing now—almost four decades later—were being sown.

One of the first things I did after the doctor's visit that confirmed my pregnancy was to make a photo collage mural. (You will be doing this same exercise later on.) The artist in me needed to celebrate this miraculous thing that was happening. On the white mural paper, I created a huge wreath of flowers cut out of magazines. Around the wreath was a poem I had written, which grew out of the mental dialogues I was having with the baby:

> *Who are you*
> *who shall call me mother,*
> *placing on my head*
> *that joyful crown*
> *tied with the love knot?*

Putting this mural up in the hall that led into our kitchen, we officially welcomed this new child who would be arriving in our home in about seven months' time. The mural was placed in the area adjacent to the range and oven. While I was cooking and preparing meals, the images and words caught my eye, nurtured my soul, and fed my heart with gratitude for the great mystery in which I was being allowed to participate. This was long before the work of David B. Chamberlin, author of *Babies Remember Birth,* long before the research on the importance of prebirth bonding. I just knew deep down inside that a relationship with a new being was unfolding in the dark, deep silence of my body and I needed to express this inner experience outwardly.

That's what you'll be doing in this chapter—expressing your inward experience outwardly, making the invisible visible, celebrating in pictures and words the mystery and sacredness of pregnancy. Someday, you may want to share with your child excerpts from the Creative Journal you are keeping at this time.

YOUR EXPECTATIONS ABOUT PREGNANCY

Just as you explored your expectations about parenting in Chapters 2 and 3, you'll be examining your expectations about pregnancy here. For it is important that you uncover the unconscious attitudes and beliefs you harbor inside your mind and heart regarding what it is like to carry a child in your body. It is also crucial that you be aware of unconscious negative beliefs and past experiences you've had with pregnancy. For these beliefs and experiences leave lasting impressions that remain in your mind, your feelings, and even the cells of your body. They can adversely affect how you approach pregnancy and birth. Some of your unconscious associations about pregnancy can even relate back to the time you were conceived.

As a therapist, I have observed numerous female clients uncover deep-seated pain and fear stemming from their own traumatic in utero experiences. When they verified with family members the circumstances around their own conception and gestation period, it became clear that these memories were accu-

rate and the fear was founded in actual events. In some in-
stances, clients who were afraid or unable to conceive learned
that their mothers had tried to abort them early on in pregnancy. After clearing their unconscious fears, many of these
women subsequently conceived and had children. Other clients
were told that there had been a real danger of miscarriage or
stillbirth when they were being carried. These traumas seem to
get stored in the cells of the body, and therapists who specialize
in body work report that clients sometimes encounter prebirth
memories.

My own experience of cellular in utero memories occurred
while getting some body work. One day, as the body therapist
worked on my lower abdominal area, I seemed to fall into a
deep black void and started shaking all over with panic. When
she asked me what I was feeling, I blurted out, "I'm hanging
onto a wall by my fingertips. I'm just barely hanging on, hanging on for dear life." I started sobbing and continued, "And
these sheets of red liquid are pouring down and threatening to
wash me out. And then I'll die."

After the session, the therapist suggested I talk to my mother
about what happened when she conceived me and what kind of
pregnancy she had. When asked, my mother told me that she'd
had trouble getting pregnant in the first place because of a
tipped uterus. After some medical treatment, she finally conceived. However, she did not know she was pregnant at first. I
was a healthy full-term baby, but I arrived a month and a half
earlier than expected. After my birth, the doctor explained this
miscalculation by saying that my mother had undoubtedly had
a period a month *after* she conceived me. They had started
counting too late. I'd never heard this story before, but it explained the utter panic I experienced in regressing to this in
utero time when I had to hang on to the "wall" of the uterus
"for dear life." My mother never conceived again. Apparently
my window of opportunity for being here was very small, and I
had to cling to it with all my might.

Our beliefs and attitudes about conception, pregnancy, and
birth can influence our lives in unimaginable ways, especially
during pregnancy. This is a time when emotions often run high,

when our bodies are going through huge changes, and we are vulnerable to unconscious influences as never before. So let's explore what pregnancy means to you in the following series of journal reflections.

Pregnancy and Me

Materials: Journal and felt pens

Purpose: To become aware of your beliefs, attitudes, and experiences associated with pregnancy; to clear negative impressions about pregnancy

Activity:

1. With your *dominant* hand, write the word *pregnant* at the top of your journal page. Free-associate by listing any words that come to mind when you think of being pregnant. Write quickly, without premeditating what you put down.

2. With your *dominant* hand, continue writing about pregnancy. Write down any thoughts or feelings that come to you. This time, use sentences.

3. With your *nondominant* hand, complete each of the following sentences as many times as you wish until you run out of things to write:
   • "What I expect from being pregnant is . . ."
   • "What scares me about pregnancy is . . ."
   • "What excites me about pregnancy is . . ."

4. With your *dominant* hand, write about the kind of pregnancy you would like to have.

YOUR PREGNANT BODY

You will probably read books and articles about health in pregnancy. Your health care professional will make recommendations about nutrition, exercise, sleep, vitamins, and so forth. In conjunction with all of this input, you can use your journal for conversing directly with your own body. Such dialogues are especially important if you have to take special tests, have discomfort or pain, or develop any complications or health problems during pregnancy. Being able to confer with your body/mind and get to the root of any emotional issues can help you deal with stress related to pregnancy.

What My Body Says

Materials: Journal and felt pens; optional: *The Picture of Health* audiotape of Dr. Capacchione's guided meditation through the body

Purpose: To learn to relax and be aware of your body sensations and physical needs; to become aware of emotions as they express themselves in your body

Activity:
1. Relax by finding a comfortable, private place where there are no distractions. Become aware of your breathing. Allow the breath to gradually become slower and deeper and to fill your belly. Put your hands on your abdomen and observe your belly moving out as you inhale. This is the natural way to breathe, the way babies instinctively breathe when they are asleep. As you inhale, experience yourself being nurtured and energized. As you exhale, shed your tensions and allow deeper and deeper relaxation.
2. Close your eyes and journey through your body. Starting with your head, sense each area as you come to it. Top of the head, back of the head, face and all the facial features, ears and jawline and neck. As you travel in your awareness through these body parts, ask yourself whether you have any strong sensations. Continue with your shoulders, arms and hands, upper back, middle and lower back, and buttocks. Then go inside your torso and check out the sensations in your chest area, heart, and lungs. Are there

any strong feelings there? Check out your stomach and digestive system, your intestines, and other abdominal organs. What sensations do you feel there? Are there any sensations in your belly? Any stirrings of life inside? Then check out your genital area and see whether there are any sensations there. Complete your body journey with your legs and feet. First one and then the other. What sensations did you discover there?

3. With your *dominant* hand, draw an outline of your body in your journal. Do a quick review of your body sensations from head to toe. If there were any areas that were broadcasting pain, stress, or discomfort, color them in on your body outline. Choose colors that represent to you the exact nature of the sensations in that body part. For instance, if an area felt hot, you might use a warm color like red or orange. If it ached, select a color that you associate with pain. There's no right or wrong way to do this. Your intuition will lead you in choosing the colors that are appropriate for you.

4. Look over your colored-in body diagram. Select the area that was in the most pain (if there was one). Write a dialogue with that body part. Using your *dominant* hand, ask the following questions: "What are you? How do you feel? Why do you feel that way? What can I do to help you?" Let your body part respond with your *nondominant* hand. You can also do this dialogue with your entire body rather than just a body part. If more than one body part was in pain or discomfort, you can dialogue with the others later.

5. Draw a picture entitled "My Healthy Pregnant Body."

HONORING YOUR PREGNANT BODY

In our society, we are constantly bombarded with portrayals of the ideal female form. Mostly it is the image of a gaunt figure with no breasts, belly, or hips. We know that many of the models and movie stars who purvey this ideal image in the media struggle with eating disorders, such as anorexia and bulimia. By

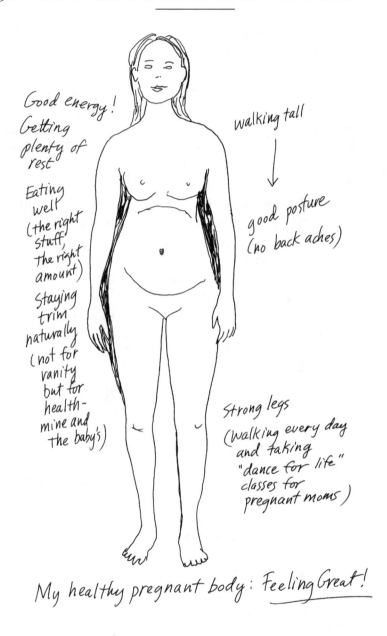

Good energy!
Getting plenty of rest

Eating well (the right stuff, the right amount)

Staying trim naturally (not for vanity but for health- mine and the baby's)

walking tall

good posture (no back aches)

Strong legs (walking every day and taking "dance for life" classes for pregnant moms)

My healthy pregnant body: Feeling Great!

their own admission, they are obsessed with cosmetic surgery, expensive "fat farms," fad diets, and programs. What is even more appalling is that girls and women everywhere try to live up to this image and do damage to their mental and physical health. They are being manipulated by media-driven, impossible standards of beauty that form the basis of a multibillion-dollar industry. This hypnotic spell exacts a high price from any girl or woman who is affected. And we are all impacted, in one way or another. It may take the form of obsessive exercising, yo-yo dieting, radical cosmetic surgery, or just plain poor self-image.

Our culture's image of the ideal female form is especially pernicious during pregnancy, for it is the antithesis of a healthy pregnant woman's body. An expectant mother's body is about roundness, abundance, a fully formed female. It's about round belly, full breasts, and hips. Pregnancy is a time for nurturing oneself and one's child, for unfolding one's womanliness, for honoring Mother Nature by partnering with her. It is not about deprivation, cinchers, girdles, precarious high heels, "abs and buns of steel." It is not about denying or camouflaging our inherent femaleness.

If you have a negative body image, pregnancy may challenge your very sense of identity. If you already thought you were too fat or too thin, too this or not enough of that, before pregnancy, this is a good time to stop and reflect upon all those old beliefs and self-put-downs. This could be your golden opportunity to surrender to your partnership with Mother Nature, to stop fighting the fact that you are in a woman's body and enjoy the blessed gift of cocreating with the source of all life. If you let it, pregnancy can open you to experience the queen within yourself. It can introduce you to the true Inner Goddess.

I am extremely grateful to my own mother for instilling in me a love for my pregnant body when I was expecting. A dressmaker by trade, she had taught me a love of beautiful clothes and how to honor the body through tasteful and personally expressive dress. One of the first things we did when I learned I was pregnant was to go shopping for clothes. In those days, A-line dresses were in style. They weren't intended for maternity wear, but they worked perfectly. We purchased two of them at a designer boutique and copied them in different fabrics and variations. Mom taught me how to sew at that time, as well, so wearing these clothes gave me a sense of real accomplishment. I felt absolutely regal during both pregnancies and experienced pregnancy as a time of creatively reinventing my own personal style. I thank my mother for handing down to me her respect for pregnancy and appreciation of a woman's pregnant body. As a result, I loved being pregnant both times. (Incidentally, you won't be surprised to hear that my mother had a very healthy and happy pregnancy when she was carrying me, and my daughter Aleta has had three healthy, happy pregnancies. This has been a very special heritage.)

Picture Me Pregnant

Materials: Journal and felt pens; collage materials

Purpose: To develop an appreciation for your pregnant body; to strengthen your body image; to become aware of your own personal style during pregnancy

Activity:

1. In your journal, with your *dominant* hand, draw a picture of your pregnant body. If you wish, look in a full-length mirror as you do this drawing. You can be fully clothed or unclothed, whichever feels more comfortable. If your Inner Art Critic jumps out and criticizes your drawing or your artistic ability, just be aware of it and keep drawing anyway.

2. Look at your drawing and write down any reactions that come to mind. How do you feel about your pregnant form?

3. If you have any negative body image about your pregnant self, write a dialogue with your body. Ask questions with your *dominant* hand, and let your body respond with your *nondominant* hand. Some suggested questions are:
   • What do you want me to do to feel better about you?
   • How can I take care of you? What kind of foods? Exercise? Other care?

4. With your *nondominant* hand, draw a picture of your outer and Inner Self. This will be an abstract or symbolic picture, not a photographically realistic portrait of what you look like in the mirror. Your outer self is how you

appear to others, your image in the world, accomplishments, roles, and tasks you perform. Your Inner Self is your private world of feelings, thoughts, experiences, wishes, and so forth.

5. Write about the picture using your *dominant* hand. What do you see there?

6. Make a magazine collage of what pregnancy looks like for you. Give it a title, like "My Pregnant Body" or "How Pregnancy Feels." How do you want to feel and dress? What do you want to do and experience? Show those things in your collage. (*Note:* You may want to get some maternity magazines so that you can include pictures of pregnant women. Beware of fashion magazines that remind you of what you do *not* look like.) Include captions and words from magazines that express the feelings and experiences you want to have.

7. Review the "Caring for Myself" exercise at the end of Chapter 4. Add to your lists with pregnancy in mind.

MEDICAL CARE DURING PREGNANCY

Health care professionals are a crucial part of your support team during pregnancy. Health care must be more than physical, however, and needs to include emotional care as well. As an expectant mother, you have a right to feel nurtured, supported, listened to, and respected by any health care professionals from whom you are receiving services. When you are shopping for an obstetrician, gynecologist, midwife, or other professional service provider, credentials, competence, and professionalism are important. Get recommendations from people you know and trust. Shop around, interview health care professionals, and ask them about their experience, their philosophy, and their values. For instance, if you want natural childbirth without overreliance on drugs, you'll need to find someone who believes as you do and can guide you on this path.

Once again, your Inner Self will be the true authority in what you decide. Through inner dialogues, you will be able to find out what is right for you. Before making your final choice about health care, be sure to consult your body and your Inner Child. If you are not happy with your health care services, use journal writing to explore what is bothering you. Find out what you want and shop around until you find it. If strong feelings are coming up, do the journal exercise "Unless Ye Become as Little Children" in Chapter 3. Scribble those feelings out so that they do not get lodged as stress in your body. The following exercise can help you make thoughtful and informed choices about health care using feelings and intuition.

Health Care, Me, and My Baby

Materials: Journal and felt pens

Purpose: To include feelings and intuition in selecting health care services; to become aware of the quality and style of health care you want

Activity:
1. With your *dominant* hand, answer the following questions:
   - Is this person or clinic respectful of me and my wishes?
   - Do I feel safe entrusting prenatal care to this person or clinic?
   - Can I ask questions comfortably, and do I get satisfactory answers?
   - Is this person or clinic competent to give me the care that I want?
2. Do a written dialogue with your Inner Child about the health care services you are receiving or considering. Write the questions with your *dominant* hand and the answers with your *nondominant* hand. Here are some questions:
   - How do you feel about [name of professional or clinic]?

- Do you feel comfortable with this person? If so, why? If not, why not?
- Do you feel safe with this person or clinic? If not, why not?
- What do you need to feel safe and comfortable with health care now?

3. With your *dominant* hand, describe the kind of pregnancy and prenatal care you want. What are your expectations? How do you want to be treated? What do you need to do to ensure that you are getting the kind of care you want?

Me: How do you feel about this new clinic we're going to since Gregory changed jobs?

Inner Child: I like the people. They're a lot nicer than the ones in that doctor's office we used to go to. Those nurses and doctors were too serious, stern and sometimes gruff. Dr. A. was always on the phone or getting interrupted by calls, and Dr. E. seemed in a hurry (when he wasn't lecturing at us, that is). We never got enough time to ask questions. I didn't feel good there and we always had to wait for hours.

Me: What do you like about the new clinic?

Inner Child: That's easy. The people smile and talk to you. I can tell they like working there. I feel welcome. And I like Dr. R. a whole lot. When I come out and say that I'm afraid about something, he listens. When I ask questions 'cause I don't understand those big words they use sometimes, he answers and explains things. He takes the time to sit and talk to me. He knows you're in a grown-up body but that I'm in here too. He knows I have feelings. Also I like the hypnotherapy he does to help us relax. He really likes kids, too. I can tell. He has a family of his own. I'm glad he's going to be there when the baby comes out. He's our friend.

The kind of pregnancy I want

I want to enjoy this pregnancy and not see it as a "sickness" or a time to be uncomfortable or limited. Sure, I'll need to make some changes, but I want to have a positive outlook. I hear other pregnant women complain about getting fat and dumpy (or they're afraid they will gain too much weight). I don't think that's inevitable and don't want it to happen to me. So I'll keep on doing what I always do: walk and dance and eat healthy food. And I'll take especially good care of myself. I do need to be sure I get enough sleep and rest so that I stay relaxed and feeling good. I don't always do that, but I really want to now—for my sake and the baby's sake.

The kind of health care I want

As far as prenatal care, I want professionals who are thoroughly competent, but most importantly who treat me with care and respect. If they're taking care of themselves, they'll have good energy and a positive attitude. That way they can create a good atmosphere for me and my baby, not just dish out a lot of medical advice routinely. I need their guidance and good, solid medical information and treatment, but *people* are important. Feelings and spirit mean as much to me as physical care. The word that keeps coming up is CARE. I want to feel cared for—physically and emotionally—and I want to care for myself and my baby.

So far, I'm pleased with the prenatal care I'm getting and so is my Inner Child. I journal with her on a regular basis to make sure her emotional and physical needs are being met. It's funny, but I feel that she is very close to the baby. The Inner Child and the baby inside: they're chums. The other day, my Inner Child told me: "If we're getting the care we want, you need to speak up and ask for what you want." Good advice!

PREGNANCY AND PARTNERSHIP

As a pregnant woman, you soon find that you are in a partnership with your unborn child. Whatever you do affects the baby; what the baby does affects you. The link is not only physical. It is deeply spiritual, mental, and emotional as well. The term *bonding* will undoubtedly come up in the literature you read about pregnancy and birth or about parenting in general. I prefer the word *partnering,* as it implies that a relationship of mutuality is established between the mother and child. This does not mean that you abdicate adult responsibility as a parent. It simply means respecting your baby's needs and balancing those with your own. As you listen to your physical and emotional needs (which you have been learning to do throughout the earlier chapters), you can begin taking responsibility for a two-way dialogue between you and your child.

The following journal exercise is intended to put you in direct contact with the spirit of the baby you are carrying. Since I do not believe that spirit is location-specific, there is no need to debate whether the baby's soul is in the fetus or not. You are free to believe whatever you wish on the subject. What I do know (based on the experience of countless clients, students, and readers) is that it is possible to converse with the baby's spirit using right-hand/left-hand dialogues. So that is what you'll be doing now.

Heart-to-Heart

Materials: Journal and felt pens

Purpose: To create a partnership with the unborn child; to establish a rapport with the spirit of the baby you are carrying

Activity:

1. With your *dominant* hand, write a love letter to your unborn child. Share the feelings in your heart. Address the child and sign it the way you would any love letter.

2. Using both hands, write a dialogue with your unborn child. Your voice (the parent) will be written with your *dominant* hand, and the voice of the unborn child will be written with your *nondominant* hand.

The other important relationship that is an integral part of pregnancy is the one with your partner or spouse. You will probably want to share your feelings regarding what it's like for you to be pregnant. Let your partner know your fears, expectations, concerns, and excitement about becoming a mother. Many mothers choose to share with their partner selected excerpts from their journal. The insights you have articulated to yourself (in this and previous chapters) are rich material for intimate sharing of this kind between parents. Your partner might even be keeping a journal and want to share feelings and insights about what it's like to be expecting a child.

If you do not have a partner at this time, journaling can help you resolve any unfinished business on the subject of relationships, partnering, or marriage. If you are judging yourself for not being in a partnership or dealing with any feelings of grief or loss, Inner Family work (Chapter 3) can help tremendously. The goal is to create your own support system (as described in Chapter 4) and create your family-by-choice. In this way, you can share both the responsibility and the joys of parenting with others who may be eager to give their love to your child.

Whether you are married, in a partnership, or single, a support system for yourself and your child during pregnancy expands the notion of partnership until it grows wider and wider. Your extended-family-by-choice will be a rich resource for you and your child.

HEALING THE PAST

If you have had negative experiences with pregnancy in the past, it is important to clear painful emotions that may be lingering on in your body and your memory. I'm referring to challenges you may have faced such as infertility, a difficult pregnancy, abortion, stillbirth, or loss of a child. The pain of these experiences can leave deep and hidden wounds that fester unless they are acknowledged and allowed to be expressed safely. For instance, many women share that they feel embarrassed talking about problems with infertility. They say things like, "I feel like I'm less of a woman," or "I feel flawed or incomplete because I haven't been able to conceive," or "I feel bad about not getting pregnant, and I know how disappointed my husband is, too." It is natural to feel sad when our dreams and hopes do not materialize, but to feel flawed or incomplete is a sign that the Inner Critic is at work.

For these women, I suggest some Inner Family work. It is important to identify critical self-talk for what it is. For women who can't get pregnant, I suggest doing journal dialogues with the Inner Child. I have found that in some cases, infertility is associated with inner conflict: the Inner Child feels it will be abandoned if the woman gives birth to a baby. I call this the "Inner Child sibling rivalry syndrome." In some cases, the woman who was thought to be infertile finally has conceived and given birth. In other cases, alternative solutions were found.

One example of this was Christine, a young professional woman who came to me for counseling. She was happily married and wanted very much to get pregnant. Unable to conceive, she and her husband had enrolled in an expensive fertility program for three in vitro fertilizations. After two attempts, Christine had still been unable to conceive. She was very anxious about the situation and sought me out to help her deal with emotional stress. We soon discovered that her Inner Child was very resistant to the idea of Christine's having a baby. The Inner Child felt that Christine worked too hard and would ignore her own needs (and her Inner Child's needs) if she had a baby. Christine's Inner Child disliked the fertility clinic's procedures, finding them cold and invasive. I suggested that Christine ease off on her preoccupation with getting pregnant and do some collages for homework. My assignment was that she make a magazine photo collage of what motherhood looked like to her. She agreed to do it.

I moved out of the area right after that, and we discontinued our sessions. A few years later, Christine attended a collage workshop I was offering at the company where she worked. As soon as she entered the room, Christine gave me a big hug and handed me a letter addressed to me at my former address. The postmark was four years old. "I tried to send this to you, but it came back," she laughed. She saw it as a sign that she was supposed to give it to me in person. The envelope contained a baby announcement with a photo of Christine, her husband, and their adopted baby boy. Christine explained that after doing the "motherhood" collage, she realized that biological birth was not so important to her but that loving and raising a child was. So she and her husband decided on adoption. She seemed to have resolved the conflict with her Inner Child as well because she looked extremely happy and couldn't stop thanking me for how I'd helped her. There was a lovely note of appreciation along with the announcement. Christine had healed her feelings of failure around pregnancy by doing some inner work. She was then able to move on and embrace parenting with all her heart.

Women who have had abortions are also in need of emotional healing. There is so much judgment on this subject, layered on top of the physical and emotional pain of terminating a pregnancy, making it very difficult for these women to heal and move on. Many women I've worked with had never talked to anyone about their abortion. There was no counseling; it was done secretly and with no emotional support whatsoever. Again, journaling with one's Inner Child and contacting one's Nurturing Parent can help tremendously in clearing these old traumas.

Women who have been raped or emotionally or physically abused also tend to have difficulty accepting pregnancy and motherhood. This is a natural reaction to an unnatural occurrence. Inner Family work is the best way I know to heal such past pain. It often needs to be done with the aid of a professional who is skilled in working with survivors of abuse. The Creative Journal method, especially exercises like the ones in Chapter 3, are being used as an adjunct to therapy with survivors. In fact, many therapists, counselors, and psychiatrists have been introduced to my work by such clients who had discovered my book *Recovery of Your Inner Child* and benefited from it.

Childbirth educators who have used my methods say that Inner Family work helps their clients who are candidates for high-risk pregnancy due to a history of abuse. In fact, many of us have observed the phenomenon that I call the "pelvic deep-freeze syndrome," a psychologically based blockage of the pelvic area that can be extremely problematic during delivery and birth. Reparenting the abused Inner Child by finding a Nurturing and Protective Parent within can help clear this blockage, both physically and emotionally, and allow for a happy and healthy pregnancy and birth.

If you've lost a child through miscarriage, Inner Family work can help you as well. Whether you want to get pregnant again, are pregnant, or will never conceive again, the process of dialoguing with your Inner Child and learning to comfort and nurture yourself will be a powerful tool for healing the past. Women who have had hysterectomies but who still want to raise a child often find that Inner Family work helps them to let go of their sorrow and grief and move toward adoption or a blended family.

If you are experiencing a difficult pregnancy, the body dialogues earlier in this chapter can be extremely valuable in helping you stay in tune with your own needs and the needs of your unborn child. Often a difficult pregnancy involves special medical procedures, tests, and visits to the doctor's office. It can be scary and frequently intimidating. Your journal can be a wonderful companion at these times, helping you to articulate your questions and concerns to share with health care professionals. I strongly urge you to reach out to your partner and your extended-family-by-choice as well. This will be good preparation for the birth of your child and enable you to receive the help that you need. I have a cousin who had a difficult pregnancy and was forced to spend many months in bed. She created a support system for herself with her computer by going on-line, frequenting chat rooms and exchanging pertinent information on bulletin boards. In this way, she counteracted feelings of isolation and informed herself about her condition and other people's experiences with the same situation. This is just one creative solution to what could have been a formidable problem.

6

Giving Birth

All the journaling and daily life application you have done so far have been preparing you for giving birth. This preparation has been *physical* (through stress reduction, breathing, body meditations, drawings, and dialogues). It has also been *emotional* and *mental* by getting you into the habit of asking yourself: "What do I want? What is my heart's desire? What are my needs? What are my values?" You've also been paving the way for birth *spiritually* by honoring yourself and your child, by becoming a more conscious and aware person and listening to your Inner Self and higher guidance. All this inner work will bear fruit in your experience of labor and childbirth.

As introspective as you have been through your journal work and other techniques, it is important to understand that birth is a time of coming out, both literally and figuratively. It is a coming out because during labor and delivery, you will need to reach out to others. You'll need the support of others—family, professionals, friends, and so forth. Birth has always involved a support system of some kind, from planning the birth to actually experiencing it. In most traditional cultures, preparation for birth and the manner of birthing were embedded in customs and practices handed down from generation to generation. In most societies, it has been expected that midwives and women relatives would attend the birth of a child. This was true throughout history and is still true in some countries and regions of the world. Even those of us living in industrialized nations have mothers and fathers who were delivered by midwives at home, as my parents were. Until recent times, childbirth was generally considered the province of women, or as my Australian Aboriginal friends say, "women's business." It was a natural process, part of the life cycle, a sacred mystery, and yet a part of everyday life and of the home environment. Babies were born in the same bed in which they were conceived. All of that changed with my generation.

BIRTH AND THE MEDICAL MODEL

In the late twenties and through the thirties, with the exception of rural areas and poor neighborhoods, America shifted to hospital births. Most people now take it completely for granted that children will be born in a hospital setting. They don't fully realize that hospital births are a very recent innovation. And they have no understanding of the deep psychological impact that hospital births have had on society and on the psyches of women, especially expectant mothers. For hospitals are generally places for the sick and dying, places where surgery, chemotherapy, and increasingly high-tech procedures are performed. By placing birth in a hospital, we have unwittingly communicated that birth is a medical procedure, is complicated, risky, and something best left to professionals. This is a medical model based in pathology and illness. As insurance companies, HMOs, and attorneys have entered the picture (including the specter of real or potential malpractice suits hovering overhead), birth has become more complicated than ever. In some hospitals, cesarean section births have almost become the norm rather than the exception.

I point all this out, not to disparage the real contribution the medical profession has made and the lives saved through truly amazing technology. We even have the technology to enter the world of the unborn child and closely observe life in the womb.

Most of this has been done with good intentions: the safety of mother and child. It is in the name of safety that some level of medical intervention has become routine in all hospital births.

However, we need to put birth into perspective. We need to counterbalance the sterility of much high-tech prenatal care and birthing by remembering always that pregnancy is not an illness or a medical condition, nor is birth a pathology to be "treated" like a malady. Although modern medical technology has provided very real lifesaving benefits, and many hospital birthing centers now have a more inviting atmosphere, the institutional setting of hospitals is unarguably *inhospitable* (interesting irony) to real "people needs."

THE BUSINESS OF BIRTH

Let's face it, the emotionally sanitized and corporate-owned modern hospital (now called a medical center; even its name has been sterilized) is not generally a soul-friendly environment. There may be some wonderful people working there, but hospitals are big businesses (as are insurance companies, HMOs, and many doctors' offices). In business-for-profit, the bottom line usually prevails. Psychological and emotional considerations and sometimes even true health issues often take a backseat. This doesn't have to be so, but it frequently is. For example, currently there is some controversy over the amount of coverage insurance companies and HMOs will allow for a woman convalescing after the birth of her child. When drugs are used (which they often are in hospitals), convalescent time is usually longer than it is after natural childbirth in a birthing center or at home. Yet many insurance companies and HMOs are severely limiting the amount of hospital days for postpartum care. I know of cases in which women who couldn't afford to pay for the extra days out of their own pockets were caught in this dilemma. Sent home too soon after a difficult delivery or cesarean section, they have suffered many complications because they simply did not have time to rest and recover in the hospital, nor did they have medical care when they needed it.

We women (and our babies) have paid a high psychological

price for the medical model of prenatal care and birthing. Just think about it. At this most intimate and life-changing event, we are taken away to an institution where we are attended by total strangers. Even if our spouse, a loved one, or a family member is there, in a hospital the professionals are in charge. It is *their* house, not ours.

There are also some rather intimidating and often uncomfortable testing procedures being administered routinely these days. They begin in pregnancy before the woman even gets to labor and birth. Some of these tests appear to be gratuitous (and expensive), and I have heard many stories of unwarranted amniocentesis and ultrasound tests that were administered without adequate justification, explanation, or preparation of the expectant mother. The emotional devastation can be immense. My daughter Aleta was told she needed such an expensive test during early pregnancy. Upon investigation, she found out that the test was totally uncalled for (given the fact that she was perfectly healthy) and would not have yielded accurate results because that particular test only works later on in pregnancy. She fired the OB-GYN and found another one who turned out to be a highly competent professional and a gem of a human being. Needless to say, she didn't have the test.

The exercises in Chapter 5 for dealing with your feelings about medical care and caregivers will help you tremendously in making decisions and choices, in learning to ask questions and insist on being included in the decision-making process. Always consult your Inner Child and your Inner Self about whether your wishes and values are being respected by health care professionals. It is your right to be consulted and educated about your options and treated like an intelligent adult.

If tests are legitimately required as your due date draws near, revisit the exercise "Health Care, Me, and My Baby" in Chapter 5. After taking any tests, process the experience in your journal. Write down your feelings about what happened for you, physically and emotionally. Did you feel intimidated or invaded by any of these procedures? If so, you may need to do some Inner Family work, comforting your Inner Child and strengthening your Protective Parent for the job of asserting yourself in further dealings with medical professionals. Use your journal as a training ground for speaking up, asking questions, and making your needs and values known. This is your right.

INFORMING YOURSELF

Of course, along with your right to participate in medical decisions, there are responsibilities. That means that you will need to investigate the various approaches to birth and postpartum care available to you. Your preferences will influence your choice of prenatal care options as well. What kind of birth do you want? Do you want to give birth in a hospital, in a birthing center, or at home? Do you want a midwife? Or do you prefer a birth attended by a hospital staff? Whom do you want present during labor and delivery? Do you want your own professional childbirth assistant with you? If you belong to an HMO, your options may be restricted. If you are having a difficult pregnancy, your choices may be somewhat limited as well. The use of medical expertise and hospital procedures may be required and should be readily available if you or your baby needs them.

I strongly urge you to take some classes, find a childbirth educator in your community and sign up for a course with her. Read some books or look at some videos about the various methods of childbirth preparation and birth. Find some mentors and people you trust who are knowledgeable about childbirth and who appreciate your values and needs. Just as there are many ways to parent a child, so, too, there are many ways to have a baby.

YOUR BIRTH SUPPORT TEAM

The journal work you have already done about building a support team will be immensely valuable in helping you answer these questions. In addition, this chapter includes activities for focusing specifically on giving birth. Regarding the building of your birth support team, let me mention a relatively recent category of childbirth professional: the *doula,* or childbirth assistant. The word *doula* comes from Greek and means "in service of." The doula acts as an aide, helping the laboring mother and her spouse, partner, or coach to concentrate on the birth of the child. A doula can bridge the gap between a parent's human needs and the hospital's policies and procedures. She can guide, translate, and interpret the often foreign language of medical jargon and technical terms so that the mother and her personal support system know what's going on.

Sometimes choices have to be made during labor, especially if unexpected conditions arise. Labor is a challenging time, for both the mother and her loved ones. It is often overwhelming to be taking in new and frequently complicated information being spoken in "medicalese" at such a time. It's very confusing to have to make a decision about something you barely understand, especially if the stakes are high. That's when a doula can be extremely helpful. She is knowledgeable about obstetric procedures, can explain options in simple language, and facilitate choice making based on your own values. Her job is to help you get your needs and your baby's needs met in a manner that fits with your values. Of course, you have to tell her in advance what is important to you and generally what kind of birth you want. Your physician or midwife needs to know what you want as well. Later on in this chapter, you'll be doing some collages and journal work that will enable you to write up your own birth plan, with clarity and with commitment to having the kind of birth experience you want. But before we do that, it is important to explore your feelings and attitudes about childbirth.

WHAT BIRTH MEANS TO ME

In Chapter 5, you did an exercise entitled "Pregnancy and Me." In it, you explored your beliefs, attitudes, and experiences associated with pregnancy. I'd like you to repeat that journal exercise, but this time replace the word *pregnancy* with *childbirth*. Again, you'll be developing awareness and clearing negative impressions, only this time the topic is birth. As you did with pregnancy, you'll be free-associating, writing thoughts and feelings, completing sentences in order to explore your expectations, fears, and excitement about giving birth. You'll also get in touch with what kind of childbirth experience you want to have. So please turn to Chapter 5 and revisit the "Pregnancy and Me" exercise, but this time with childbirth in mind.

CHILDBIRTH: A CELEBRATION OF LIFE

When you fully answer the question "What kind of birth experience do I want?" you are taking responsibility for welcoming your baby into the world. When you do this, you strengthen yourself and create a strong partnership with the baby. Imagine being born with the knowledge that your mother (father or members of the birth support team) cared enough to choose how they wanted to welcome you. That they went to the effort to choreograph the big event to the best of their ability. That they held your birth as a sacred moment to be cherished and planned for creatively and thoughtfully.

Birth can be scary, and it can also be glorious, a true celebration of life. Fear of the unknown causes anxiety in many expectant parents. Empowering yourself with information, knowledge, and the support of experienced people can turn fear into joyful anticipation. It can mean the difference between being a passive recipient of health care services and becoming an active participant in the experience of welcoming your child into the world. The combination of going out for information and support and going within (through Creative Journaling) for guidance from the Inner Self has proved extremely effective in empowering pregnant women and expectant couples. Childbirth educators using this method report that moms and dads are indeed experiencing childbirth as a celebration. This is even true for women who are abuse survivors and have had to do a lot of Inner Family healing.

I've been told by childbirth educators and new parents that this method was truly empowering and enabled the parents to take charge of their child's birth instead of abdicating to the professionals. As one young mother said, "I realized that all the professionals and my support system were there to assist me, not the other way around, the way I had been trained to believe.

I put myself, my husband, and my baby at the center of things. We asked for what we wanted, and we got it!"

Perhaps the most dramatic experiences I've had of both parents and child being at "the center of things" was at the birth of my first grandchild. My daughter Aleta was a thoughtful consumer of health care services during her pregnancy and during the birth as well. Upon realizing that she was probably pregnant, she called many doctors to ask them a few questions over the phone before making an appointment. She wanted to know about their philosophy, policies, and procedures. Most of them wouldn't even answer her questions. As mentioned earlier in the chapter, the first OB-GYN she visited started prescribing expensive tests right away. Aleta went home and researched these tests only to find that they were totally inappropriate considering her excellent health and the early stage of her pregnancy. She never went back to his office.

The next OB-GYN she called returned her call one evening and talked to her for quite a while, answering her questions in depth. She immediately sensed his dedication and that their philosophies were compatible. He became her obstetrician during pregnancy, and he delivered the baby. Before going into labor, Aleta choreographed the birth as meticulously as a theater director. She selected whom she wanted present and what each person's assignments would be. Her husband was there for moral and physical support. Her best friend, who had attended childbirth classes with Aleta, was her breathing coach during labor. I was the presiding grandmother and official photographer. Aleta's sister, Celia, flew out from New York to be present and take care of any communications with the hospital staff and with our other family members who were waiting anxiously at home. Another chum of Aleta's was our all-purpose helper, going out for food and beverages, running errands, and taking care of miscellaneous tasks.

Labor took place in a special childbirth pavilion at Santa Monica Hospital. The room was large and pleasant—not the typical cold, sterile hospital setting. There was a big rocking chair in the corner, artwork on the walls, and furnishings that resembled a home rather than an institution. The hospital staff were warm, highly competent, and very accepting of Aleta's formidable support team, which later included her chiropractor, who came in to do special adjustments during labor.

Although it was a long labor, which is fairly typical for first births, we all worked together as an extended family team and Aleta received the support she wanted from those with whom she felt most comfortable. It was a truly joyful experience for all of us. Aleta knew what kind of birth she wanted to give her child, and she got it. You can, too, if you know what you want and know that you and your child deserve to have it.

In the next journal exercise, you'll be picturing exactly what you value and desire regarding the birth of your child. This collage will be your visual affirmation and provide a graphic blueprint for your written birth plan, to be created later in this chapter.

Blueprint for Birth

Materials: Journal and felt pens; collage materials

Purpose: To portray the kind of childbirth you want for yourself and your child; to clarify your values, needs, and wishes regarding childbirth

Activity:

1. On a large sheet of art paper or poster board, create a photo collage of childbirth. You can use magazine photos, snapshots, and other picture materials. Include appropriate captions and phrases from magazines. You may want to draw images or symbols and write your own words as well. Use whichever hand you like for drawing and writing. Picture the birthing experience you want.

2. In your journal, with your *dominant* hand, write impressions about what you see in your collage.

3. Write a dialogue with your unborn child and ask the baby what he or she wants regarding labor and birth. Let your *dominant* hand ask the questions and your *nondominant*

hand answer for the baby. Include your baby's wishes in your collage, in the form of phrases or pictures or images.

4. Put your collage up where you can see it frequently. Reinforce this positive image on a daily basis by looking at it as often as possible. Consider this your "visual affirmation."

CREATING A BIRTH PLAN

In order to communicate your needs and wishes regarding childbirth to your support system, you'll have to articulate them in words. An excellent way to do this is to write a birth plan. You can draft one in your journal and then give a photocopy to the appropriate people—professionals, your partner, friends or family members who may be present at the birth, and so on.

My Birth Plan

Materials: Journal and felt pens

Purpose: To clarify your values, needs, wishes, and goals regarding how you give birth to your child; to write a first draft of your birth plan

Activity:

1. With your *dominant* hand, write a couple of pages describing the kind of birth you want to give your child. What are your feelings about giving birth? What is your philosophy about childbirth? What kind of setting do you want? Whom would you like to be present at your child's birth? How would you like to be treated? What kind of support do you want from your partner or other members of your support system? What other concerns and needs do you have? Be specific.

2. After doing research into childbirth procedures, using your *dominant* hand, write a list of what you want in each of the following categories:

- Labor
- Birth
- Postpartum care
- Special procedures (if appropriate or needed)
- Nursery care for your baby

In each of these categories, be specific. Include such labor concerns as freedom of movement, fetal monitoring devices, medication and anesthesia, preparation procedures (such as shaving of pubic hair and enemas), use of I.V. liquids during labor and delivery, surgical procedures (such as episiotomies), and so on. Many of these procedures are routine, but you and your doctor (if it is a hospital birth) can discuss which ones are optional, advisable or essential (given your special needs), or completely unnecessary. Visit the hospital where you are going to deliver your baby and find out what its standard procedures are before you complete this journal entry. The main point is to express your wishes and needs in your journal. Be sure to detail your wishes regarding the treatment of your baby as well. Are you planning to breast-feed? Do you want rooming-in, if that is an option?

3. Rewrite your birth plan and make a copy for whomever you want to include in your birth support team. Be sure to discuss your birth plan thoroughly with your doctor or midwife. If it will be a hospital birth, ask your doctor to sign a copy and have a copy on file at the hospital where you will be delivering the baby. If your doctor arrives at the hospital after you do, the staff will have this birth plan to refer to regarding your preferences. Take a copy with you as well.

Remember that no plan is written in concrete. You will need to be flexible in dealing with health care professionals, institutions, agencies, and the like. You may need to negotiate certain points and to have an alternate plan regarding some issues. Doctors, nurses, hospitals, and HMOs have to follow certain regulations and laws. But many of their guidelines are just that and can be altered to meet your needs and preferences, especially if you get your doctor's support and signature on your birth plan.

If you don't know what you want, there's no way you'll ever get it. By being clear enough to ask questions and to communicate your needs and preferences to others, your chances of having a truly empowering and fulfilling birth experience are greatly increased. The idea is to give you the greatest freedom of choice possible in having the kind of childbirth experience you want. You and your baby deserve this, and you have a right to it.

THE JOY OF BIRTH

The recovery period after the birth of a child can yield some rich and memorable journal entries. There are many moments that you will want to treasure for years to come. I strongly recommend that you keep your journal nearby as a special companion on this next step of the journey into parenthood. Revisit some of the earlier exercises in this book. Draw, scribble, and write your feelings out. Record your experiences and insights.

Write a love letter to your baby with your *dominant* hand. Dialogue with your baby as you did when you were pregnant. What does he or she need? Ask with your *dominant* hand, and write the answer with your *nondominant* hand.

I'd also suggest writing a thank-you letter to the Creator for the great gift you've been given. Write thank-you notes to your support team as well, your partner, assistants, family members, and professionals who were there for you during labor, delivery, and beyond. You may want to draft these notes in your journal and then copy them out and send them. These journal entries will be especially sweet to look back on in years to come and may be something to share with your child later on.

GUIDANCE FROM THE INNER SELF

Now that your baby is here, ask your Inner Self or Higher Power for guidance in loving and cherishing this new life that has been entrusted into your care. Ask for guidance, and it shall be given to you. This is a journal activity that yields the most fruit when done on a regular basis.

Journaling is a wonderful way to celebrate the joyful moments, to express gratitude, to cherish experiences of being a parent. If you have any concerns, fears, or difficult feelings, you can also bring them to the altar of your Inner Self. When you are in doubt, feeling insecure, regretting something you have or have not done for your child, using your journal to explore your feelings and asking for wisdom and solace can help you tremendously. Remember, you are human, and you will face challenges, make mistakes, and learn lessons. But there is also a spark of the divine in you. It lives in your own heart. Go there and bask in it, bathe in it, and find healing within.

CIRCUMSTANCES BEYOND YOUR CONTROL

In childbirth, as in life, no matter how much we plan or try to predict outcomes, we must always understand that things might not turn out exactly as we had wanted. Sometimes complications arise for mother or child or both. For instance, I've known many perfectly healthy women who took excellent care of themselves in pregnancy, prepared thoughtfully and thoroughly for natural childbirth, and then were surprised by last-minute circumstances that arose requiring an emergency cesarean section delivery. Some of these women have told me that they experienced great sorrow and feelings of loss.

"I felt like I was robbed of something," Cynthia, a young mom, told me. "I know the baby was healthy, and I was thrilled about that. Yet I felt lots of depression and sadness about the way the baby was born. I had really wanted a natural birth. I know it was essential for my health and the baby's to have the C-section, and yet I can't deny my grief over it." Using her journal to explore her feelings helped her to heal her sadness and disappointment. She eventually got pregnant again, joined a support group for VBAC (vaginal birth after cesarean) and had her second child naturally without any surgical intervention.

Despite advanced medical research, scientific knowledge, and a plethora of high-tech tools, there are still risks associated with birth. That will always be so. Mother Nature is a formidable force who teaches us to put ourselves and our technology into perspective. Complications are still possible. These can range from cesarean section delivery and premature birth to temporary infant illness or handicaps (including some that can be treated and remedied and others that cannot). Sometimes a child needs prolonged care in an incubator and cannot be taken home for some time.

Unexpected outcomes remind us that a Higher Power is really in charge and that this Higher Power is our silent partner in childbirth and in everyday life. You can call this Higher Power whatever you like: God, the Creator, Holy Spirit, Universal Mind, the Source, the Force. The name doesn't matter, but the experience of its presence does. And it matters most when you are confronted with circumstances beyond your control.

If you encounter any disappointments, losses, or complications during labor or delivery or shortly afterward, I urge you to turn to your silent partner or Higher Power for solace, support, and strength. Even if you don't run into complications, I strongly recommend that you enter labor with a prayer on your lips and in your heart. For childbirth is one of *the* peak experiences in life, a time when you will be plunged into the mystery of life and death, darkness and light, pain and joy. No matter what the outcome, this experience will change you forever. Surrender yourself to this power that is so much greater than yourself and let it care for you and your child. Then, no matter what the outcome, you will know that it was meant to be. Call it fate, destiny, karma, or whatever you like. It is not in your hands but in the hands of the Creator of all life.

Prayer to the Creator

Materials: Journal and felt pens

Purpose: To write your own prayer to your Higher Power or the Divine as you experience it; to have faith in and surrender to divine providence

Activity:

1. Write a prayer of thanksgiving, expressing your appreciation for all that you have been given. Say what it is you are grateful for and how it has blessed your life.

2. Write a prayer of supplication to the Creator of all life or to your Higher Power using whatever name feels right for you. In your prayer, allow any worries, fears, or doubts to pour out. Ask for help, comfort, and guidance. Ask for courage and wisdom and to see love's light, even in the darkest moments.

7

Adoption, Stepparenting, and Blended Families

Children come to us for parenting in many ways other than through biological birth. Some people welcome children into their lives through adoption or through marriage or partnership with someone who is already a parent. The adopted child may come as an infant, a toddler, or older. The stepchild usually comes at an older age because of death or divorce from a biological or adoptive parent. Sometimes, the stepparent becomes the legal guardian as well. In this chapter, we'll explore all these ways of becoming a parent. As in previous chapters, you'll be using your journal to explore feelings, beliefs, attitudes, expectations. Through collage and writing, you'll have an opportunity to creatively map your own unique experiences and wishes.

ADOPTION

WHEN YOU ADOPT A CHILD

I will begin by admitting openly that I have not had direct personal experience with legal adoption. However, I have had many, many close friends, numerous clients and students, and some in-laws who have adopted children. I have assisted many of these people through the process and am grateful that they shared their experiences with me. They were the ones who taught me that journaling and collage work can be a godsend during the highs and lows of the initial adoptive process as well as the day-to-day caring for and loving an adopted child.

It only stands to reason that taking over the parental role for another person's biological child will be complex. In our society, it involves legal, emotional, and health issues we have never faced before. For instance, many young mothers who give their children up for adoption are unhealthy, may not have had prenatal care, or may be addicted to alcohol, drugs, or other substances. Babies born with fetal alcohol syndrome or related conditions are usually affected for the rest of their lives. Consequences range from chronic health problems to learning disabilities and mental disorders. Adoptive parents can inherit even more serious problems if the birth mom was on "crack," living a chaotic lifestyle, or abusing her child. You need to be forewarned, especially in the case of older children, whose scars tend to go deeper and last longer. Children who are adopted when they are older may suffer from the emotional scars of years of abuse or neglect and may engage in all kinds of acting-out behavior. Although these early formative conditions were not created by the adoptive parents, they and the child are the ones who have to live with the consequences.

I know a couple who were childless for years and then decided to adopt two girls, ages four and two. The children, who had been severely malnourished both physically and emotionally, were in a foster home. The couple were fully aware that the birth mother had been on drugs and did not receive prenatal care. However, the couple loved these children and adopted them, knowing full well that there were going to be emotional and health challenges ahead. There were some legal battles in store as well, as the birth mom tried to get her children back. The birth mother was so obviously unfit that the courts did the right thing and ruled in favor of the adoptive couple. Severe limitations on visitations were mandated by the judge, and many conditions were imposed, such as having the visits supervised by another adult at all times.

The point is that this adoptive couple made an informed choice. They knew what they were getting into and were willing to embrace these children as their own, in spite of the risks and challenges. As the adoptive mom said to me, "These kids just got to our hearts. It was like falling in love. We couldn't walk out on them. And my husband has become a different person. He's softer, and yet he's firm with them, too. I never knew what a truly loving man he was until now." She paused and then added, "Don't get me wrong. It's been *really* hard, especially the legal fight. But the kids are doing so much better. That's our real reward. We don't regret a thing."

This couple were mature and dedicated. They are also realistic enough to know that there is some damage that may never be reversed, and they aren't about to play "savior." That is a dangerous temptation, especially for those who tend to be codependent. Do not think you can change or fix a child. Anyone who is adopting out of a need to "fix" a child has trouble in store. The point is to go in with your eyes and heart open. This takes a great deal of maturity and strength.

Other concerns for those who are adopting revolve around the birth parent. We've all heard or read stories about the heart-wrenching dilemma of parents whose child was later claimed by the biological parent (usually the mother). Shocking tales of heated legal battles between birth moms or surrogate mothers and adoptive parents have made the headlines and been featured in TV specials, either in a journalistic or dramatic portrayal. As one adoptive mother told me, "I can't watch those shows. It's my worst nightmare—that Timmy's birth mom would suddenly appear at our door and snatch or legally get our child away from us."

The legal aspects of adoption have become a hot issue. Laws have been tested, made, or changed as a result of sometimes bizarre and unprecedented situations involving birth parents or surrogate mothers and those who are trying to adopt the child. I have learned a lot from adults who were adopted as infants or children and have joined the growing movement of adults who are seeking their biological parents. Many have had a joyful reunion with birth parents; others have been rejected by their parents yet again and had to learn to live with that fact. Still others have never found their biological parents no matter how hard they tried. I have great compassion for these adult adoptees and have been very pleased to hear that Creative Journal work helped them tremendously in listening to their true feelings, in following their heart, and in accepting whatever happened as a result. The right-hand/left-hand dialogues with their birth parents (dead or alive, found or not found) have been an especially powerful aid in their healing.

I see the same benefits from journaling for adults who are planning to adopt a child or have already done so. Adoption is not an easy decision, nor is it one to be made without being fully informed. As one adoptive mother said, "One thing I can say to my child that many biological parents can't say is, 'You were chosen. We really wanted you. There was no mistake about it.' When you consider how many babies are unwanted mistakes—resulting from careless sex or a woman's trying to hold on to a man by getting pregnant—we feel that choosing our child was a gift that we gave her. Of course, she's been a true gift to us, too."

In my counseling work, I have observed that this "choosing of a child" is indeed a precious gift, especially to a baby or youngster who has been given up by her birth parents for whatever reason. It takes a lot of courage to adopt a child. It has its own unique set of challenges. For instance, sometimes an adopted child feels angry about having to be separated from his biological parents (regardless of the circumstances). He may vent his anger on those who are closest at hand—the adoptive parents. We will explore this issue later on through journal exercises for communicating with your adopted child. I also recommend that you consider introducing your older adopted children to journaling. My books *The Creative Journal for Children* and *The Creative Journal for Teens* provide exercises for youngsters starting as young as five and going up to nineteen.

We'll begin here with a journal exercise that can be used for those of you in the process of adopting as well as those who are considering it. As you've done in previous chapters, you'll be exploring your feelings and attitudes. You'll also be addressing the issues that commonly come up before or after adoption.

This exercise will be familiar because one or another version of it has been included in previous chapters. It is an all-purpose method for tuning in on how you feel and think, what you want and need regarding any aspect of parenting (or of your life).

How I Feel

Materials: Journal and felt pens

Purpose: To become aware of your beliefs, attitudes, and experiences associated with adoption; to approach adoption by being clear and informed

Activity:

1. With your *dominant* hand, write the word *adoption* at the top of your journal page. Free-associate by listing any words that come to mind when you think of adopting a child. As you did before in earlier exercises like this one, write quickly and avoid premeditating what you write.

2. With your *dominant* hand, continue writing about adoption. Write down in sentences your thoughts or feelings about adoption. How will your life be changed after you adopt? What will you need to do to include a child in your life, your marriage, or your partnership? How will adopting a child affect your relationships with your partner, family of origin? Friends? Work? Other?

3. With your *nondominant* hand, complete each of the following sentences as many times as you wish until you run out of things to write:
   - "What I expect from adopting a child is . . ."
   - "What scares me about adopting a child is . . ."
   - "What excites me about adopting a child is . . ."

4. Draw a vertical line down your journal page or use two pages side by side. Head the left side "Risks" and the right side "Rewards." With your *dominant* hand, fill in each

column, listing the pluses and minuses of adoption at this time. On another page, write about the risks and benefits in sentences, still using your *dominant* hand.

5. With your *nondominant* hand, write about your biggest concerns regarding adoption. Include such issues as physical and emotional health of the child, legal procedures and protection, your support system, change in lifestyle, work, impact on your relationship with your partner or other loved ones, the child's relationship with his or her birth parents.

6. Make a collage called "Adoption." Using magazine photos, snapshots, or other images, create a visual affirmation of the adoption you want. With your *dominant* hand, write about the kind of experience you would like to have if you want to adopt or have already begun the process.

Note: If any unresolved issues about infertility or the inability to give birth to a child come up while doing this exercise, journaling can help. With your *dominant* hand, write in free association (as in step 1 above) on the subject of infertility or whatever word you want to use. Write down your feelings as well, using your *nondominant* hand.

PEOPLE AND PROCEDURES

Dealing with adoption procedures is a lot like dealing with health care professionals during pregnancy. You need to know what you want from any professionals who are involved in helping you with the process of adoption, such as attorneys, social workers, agency representatives, counselors, and physicians. Find out how much protection you have regarding the birth parents' suddenly wanting the child back. It happened to a friend of mine after only two days with the infant. She and her husband were heartsick over it. For that reason, some adopt children from foreign lands and even different cultures. There are agencies that specialize in such adoptions.

No matter where you seek to adopt your child, be informed about your legal rights. Research the professionals you are

In thinking about adoption I realize that there is a lot of insecurity. We don't know when we'll get the baby, as it is a private adoption. We're always on pins and needles about when a baby will be available for us. And I really hated the invasiveness of the adoption agency interviews (or should I call them the 3rd degree). They scrutinized everything about us almost as if we were criminals. I realize they have to protect the baby involved, but nevertheless we felt we were under a microscope. All we want to do is love and care for a child, but the agency process seemed to create an atmosphere of criticism and cold bureaucracy. It ran counter to the whole idea of nurturing a child.

Also, I realize that we've been married for nine years and have a lifestyle that has not included children, especially an infant. Young couples who just got married and are having a baby right away never got settled in a "couples only" way of life. Within a year of getting married they are parents and since they knew they were having a baby on a specific date they've been able to plan for it. That's been a problem for us. It's hard to plan. We've had to be very flexible, but I guess that's good preparation for becoming a parent.

When we get the baby, we will need to change a lot of things. We're used to going out at night at the drop of a hat. But now we'll have to plan ahead and find a baby-sitter. And babies get sick sometimes so Greg and I will have to be flexible. In planning to do things—just the two of us—we'll have to take the baby into account. And we'll be doing more things that we can include the baby in, too. We've also decided to change our work schedules so that one of us can be with the baby as much as possible. Fortunately, we are in jobs that allow that, especially since Greg is self-employed now. And my boss is fine with flex time. As far as family goes, I know our parents will want to spend time with the baby so I guess that will have to be factored in. Since none of them live here, either they or we will be traveling. I'd prefer that they come visit us at first. Traveling long distances with a small baby isn't my idea of a great time and I'd think it would be hard on the baby, too.

The thing that scares me the most about adopting is: Will we be able to keep the baby? What if the mother changes her mind? What if she comes back and wants the baby before she's signed the adoption papers? It feels like we'll just be in the position of baby-sitters or foster care parents until that paper is signed. What if we really bond with the baby and then it is taken away? That really worries me. I know it can happen—it HAS happened lots of times. I just saw a case on the news recently about a mother who came back and she did get the child.

The other thing that concerns me is: Will the baby be healthy? Did the mother drink, smoke, or use drugs while she was pregnant? Will we be taking on problems caused by someone else's negligence? When my cousin Jen adopted Tommy he was a very normal looking, happy child. But when he got older he had learning disabilities and in his teens he drank and used drugs. Jen and her husband rarely drink and never did drugs. But Tommy's natural mother was an alcoholic. I'm concerned that we might end up in the same boat.

working with thoroughly. What are their credentials? How were you referred to them? Did you know them already? Do you feel genuinely comfortable with them? Are you getting your needs met and your questions answered adequately?

You'll also want to check in with your Inner Child and your highest inner wisdom, to see whether you trust those who are assisting you in the adoption. Do a right-hand/left-hand dialogue with your Inner Child, as you did in Chapter 3. Also do one with your Inner Self or wisdom guide. In both cases, your voice writes with your *dominant* hand, and the child or wisdom guide writes with your *nondominant* hand.

Think of everyone helping with the adoption as your support team. If they don't seem to be helping but hindering, confusing you, or in any way behaving in a condescending manner, you'll need to deal with that, both internally and externally. Use the journal exercise in Chapter 4 entitled "My Support Team."

Clarify who is on your team and what each member is doing. You deserve to be treated with respect, honesty, and a cooperative attitude. As mentioned earlier, one hears horror stories of what happens later down the line, often because of some legal glitch or lack of clarity during the adoption procedures. Much of this can be prevented through thoughtfulness on your part and through being selective about who helps you with the adoption. Be sure you know what you want and are getting it.

Risks and Rewards

Materials:　Journal and felt pens; collage materials

Purpose:　To listen to your Inner Child's feelings about your adoption support team; to tap into your inner wisdom about adopting a child

Activity:

1. Write a dialogue with your Inner Child. Use your *dominant* hand to ask the questions and your *nondominant* hand to answer from your Inner Child. Ask your Inner Child how it feels about the adoption. Does it want a child in your life? Is it getting its own needs met? If not, how can you better meet those needs? Ask your Inner Child to tell you what it needs from you to feel comfortable about the adoption.

2. With your *nondominant* hand, draw a picture in your journal of your adoption support team. This includes anyone who is providing procedural guidance, mentoring, technical or legal support, access to adopting a child in any way. Write in the names of these individuals or groups. With your *dominant* hand, write out your feelings about the members of your support team. What's working for you? What's not working? Are there any people you want to add to or remove from your team? After writing this, share your insights and needs with your partner or most significant member of your support team.

3. With your *dominant* hand, write a prayer to your Inner Self or Higher Power or God (whatever name you prefer) asking for guidance and courage in the adoption process and what lies ahead.

4. Write a dialogue with your Inner Self or Higher Power. With your *dominant* hand, describe all your feelings and concerns about adoption. Ask for guidance and love or anything else you need at this time. With your *nondominant* hand, allow your Inner Self or Higher Power to respond.

THE ADOPTION TRIANGLE: YOU, THE CHILD, AND THE "OTHER PARENTS"

There is an *emotional* triangle involved in adoption, regardless of whether you or your child ever see the birth parents. The birth parents *do* exist, and even if they are out of sight, they may not be out of mind. This will certainly be true for older children who remember their birth parents. Yet it may be just as true for children who never knew them.

One adoptive mother told me she never thought much about her child's birth mother for the first couple of years. The circumstances of the adoption were such that there was never a possibility the woman might show up. Then one day, when her son was about three, it happened. "I can remember it clearly," she told me. "He was sitting in the bathtub and suddenly asked, 'What do you think my mom is like?' In that moment, the woman became real to me. I gave it some thought and then told him that I felt she must be a very special person to have had such a very special child. I really do believe that and am very grateful to her for bringing our son into the world."

For some adoptees, asking questions about their birth parents doesn't become a burning issue until they are adolescents or adults. As one young mom told me:

There was something about getting pregnant that somehow got me thinking about my own birth. I never thought I'd want to contact my biological mother. In fact, I was always pissed off that she gave me up for adoption. I didn't want to know a woman who would do that. But the more I thought about it, I realized I hadn't given her a chance. I guess being pregnant and having a baby got me thinking how awful it would be to lose a child, for any reason. When I found her, I felt so much compassion. She had not wanted to give me up. Her parents forced her to, and she still carried grief and guilt for not having stood up for herself and me. We both did a lot of healing.

Another man (who was adopted at birth) did some collages of his life story. When he did journal work about being born, he had a profound breakthrough in relation to his birth mother. As a child, when he was told about being adopted, he developed a deep resentment for this woman who had "thrown her baby away," as he described it. He said he had felt like refuse, unwanted and unloved by her, and had harbored hatred in his heart for years. It had negatively affected all of his relationships with women (of which there had been many). While doing a journal dialogue with his birth mom, this middle-aged man began sobbing uncontrollably. What the spirit of his birth mother told him in the dialogue was that she had loved him deeply and giving him away was the hardest thing she ever had to do. As a poor, unwed mother with no means of support or help, she knew she could not provide for her child. She wanted what was best for him, so she found a good family to raise him. Too heartbroken about losing her child, she could not bring herself to stay in touch with the adoptive parents or with her son.

I share these stories because, no matter who the birth mother or parents are, they did in fact bring your adopted child into the world. It is important to accept the fact that without them, you wouldn't have your son or daughter to raise and to love. We don't have to accept or approve of their lifestyle or their decisions, but we can feel compassion for any birth parent who must give his or her child up for whatever reason. As a therapist, I have witnessed the deep soul sadness these birth parents and children carry with them. The important thing is that you accept the *existence* of all those connected to the child and learn to communicate with everyone involved—your partner, your child (and even the birth parents through journal dialogues, if that is appropriate).

COMMUNICATING ABOUT ADOPTION

The first line of communication in adoption is with yourself. The next link is with your partner or coparent, if you have one. Then there's the connection that needs to be made with the child (even before he or she is found or comes into your life). The other link is with the birth parents.

Journaling has provided a readily accessible vehicle for communicating with yourself. And communicating with a spouse or partner is easy because the person is there and you can talk to him or her. You can share your feelings about the adoption, discuss your fears, disappointments, enthusiasm, and moments of joy. If communication breaks down between you and your partner on the subject of adoption (or anything else, for that matter), *a good technique for clearing conflict or confusion is to do a journal dialogue using both hands.* You've done them before in earlier chapters. As always, the *dominant* hand writes for your voice, and the *nondominant* hand writes for the other person. In this way, you are likely to gain insight not only about your own feelings but about the other person's as well. I believe there is a strong spiritual connection that happens in these dialogues. Call it a soul-to-soul chat. I have seen this journal process work wonders in so many lives and so many relationships.

The last person most adoptive parents try to communicate with before their child comes to them is the *child* himself or herself, especially if they adopt an infant. We think that we can't talk to infants and that they certainly wouldn't understand or be able to talk to us. And we are sure that we can't communicate with someone who isn't there yet (as in cases when the infant or child hasn't arrived in our home). How can we talk to someone who isn't there? The same way we did with the birth parent—through a right-hand/left-hand dialogue. People who want to adopt but haven't found a child yet can even do journal dialogues with the child who is waiting for them somewhere in the world. Again, your voice writes through the *dominant* hand, and the child's voice (in this case, the child or child-spirit) writes with the *nondominant* hand. It's all about soul communication, Inner Self to Inner Self. You can make the connection anytime in your journal.

After the child is in your life, you can do the same kind of dialogue. It's helpful to do a right-hand/left-hand dialogue with your infant or toddler who can't speak yet, especially if the child is ill or chronically fussy. This is a whole other frequency of conversing, and the insights you'll gain are likely to blow your mind. At the same time, your heart will feel the truth that is spoken, and your soul will know you have indeed communicated with the child at the deepest level of spirit. One mother did a journal dialogue with her colicky three-month-old and got some information about specific nutritional needs that weren't being met. The baby's voice spoke through the *nondominant* hand, and she spoke through her *dominant* hand. As soon as she changed the baby's formula, he became happy and content. You can also write a love letter to your adopted child in your journal, using your *dominant* hand. This is a wonderful heart-opener and will certainly bring you closer together.

For adoptive parents, communication with the birth parent is a sensitive issue for reasons already discussed. Perhaps they don't know who the birth parents are and will never know. Maybe they are angry that the birth parents abandoned or abused the child and don't want to know who they are or have anything to do with them (even in their journal). Meet them or not, the birth parents are present in your child's body and mind as an invisible force. The child may resemble the parents or have inherited certain talents or personality traits. And an adopted child cannot help but wonder about his or her birth parents. This is normal and natural.

If you have unresolved issues about the birth parents of your child, journaling can come in very handy. The right-hand/left-hand journal dialogue is a powerful way to gain insight into the "other parents" and to express your gratitude to them for bringing your adopted child into the world. If you are harboring judgment or anger for any reason, this technique can lead you to a natural forgiveness. Don't force it; just let it happen in its own time.

NURTURING THE RELATIONSHIP WITH YOUR PARTNER

Taking on the role of parenting brings both joys and stress. This is just as true for birth parents who raise their own children as it is for adoptive parents. Sometimes, however, the stress of adopting can be more challenging. There may be expensive legal battles, a birth parent may show up unannounced, or the child might start acting out based on earlier traumatic experiences with a birth parent or in a foster home. Remember the couple who adopted the two children of the dope-addicted birth mother? Making a home for these two children could have stressed their relationship beyond the limit, but they didn't let it. In fact, some adoptive couples do get divorced—in some cases, because their existing problems are aggravated by the stresses of adoption; in other cases, simply because their relationship is not working out.

During times that are especially stressful, pay close attention to nurturing yourself and your relationship with your partner. I recommend counseling, support groups, and journal work. Here are some journal suggestions:

- *Return to exercises in Chapters 3 and 4 for self-nurturing.* You might want to suggest to your partner that he or she do some journaling *à deux* in which you each do your own journal work and then share any insights that would help foster communication between the two of you.
- *Do some right-hand/left-hand dialogues with your partner in your journal,* making a soul connection before trying to resolve a problem area face-to-face. Again, your *dominant* hand writes your voice, your *nondominant* hand speaks for your partner. Some partners even read their dialogues to each other. Use your own judgment about this. The key factors are safety, truth, and love.

- *Write a love letter to your partner telling what you appreciate and admire about him or her.* This letter can then be copied out and sent and can help tremendously in building a bridge between you.
- *Make a list of things you can do to nurture your relationship.* Then be sure to *do* them. Making the list isn't enough. Walk your talk.

LIFESTYLE CHANGES

Many adoptive parents have a firmly established lifestyle before a child comes into their lives. They may have been married for several years before they realized they would not be giving birth to a child and decided to adopt. An individual who is adopting may have a career and activities based on being single and free of the responsibility of child care. One adoptive mom joked about her rude awakening the first time she stumbled into the need to shift her lifestyle. "After our adopted child came to us, the first time my husband and I were going out for the evening, I realized at the last minute that I had completely forgotten something—a baby-sitter! I simply had never had to think about that before. That was a real shock." Welcome to Adoptive Parenting 101.

COMMUNICATING ADOPTION TO THE CHILD

One of the most sensitive areas of communication between some adoptive parents and children will be telling the child he or she is adopted. Again, the key factors are safety, truth, and love. When, where, and how to tell your child that he or she was adopted is strictly up to you. (Of course, if you got the child when he or she was older, this won't be an issue. The child knows you are not the birth parents.)

How much or how little you share about the circumstances of the adoption and birth parents is an individual choice, too. *If you are having any problems telling your child he or she is adopted, I would suggest writing a letter to your child in your journal before talking face-to-face.* Using your *dominant* hand, express how you feel about him or her and about the adoption.

Write from your heart. If it's difficult for you, admit that in your journal letter. Just tell the truth. You don't have to worry about your child's reaction in this journal entry. It's for your eyes only. Just convey your feelings—with safety, truth, and love.

In discussing the birth parent with your child, it is important to be as kind and compassionate as possible. But you can't fake this one. If you've come to some deep insights and understanding through the journal dialogues, it will be easier for you. Bad-mouthing a birth parent only tends to make the child feel bad about him- or herself. Children conclude: "My mother [or father] was no good, and so I must be no good, too." This same principle applies in divorce, which we will discuss later. Nothing is served by making children feel that the person who brought them into the world is totally worthless. Think about it. How would you feel?

I will close this section on adoption by quoting a young mother of two adopted kids:

> To those considering adoption, I say, "Go for it!" It changes your life so much. You see things differently. Without kids, couples or individuals can tend to focus just on themselves. With kids, there's a shared focus—on the kids and on a much larger world. It definitely changes your perspective and broadens your horizons. I even had my own toy store for awhile—all because I had two kids. I never would have done that before.

She went on to talk about the important role their religion had played in their lives. "We got involved in the church for our kids' sake, we thought. But now my husband and I are really into it, and what a difference that has made."

STEPPARENTING

As the divorce rate has increased over the past three decades, stepparenting has become more and more commonplace. Many childless individuals are marrying or moving in with partners who have children from a former marriage. In addition to adjusting to the marriage or partnership, there is the added factor of adjusting to parenthood right away. There's no nine months of pregnancy, no period of adoption in which to prepare. The child or children are part of the package right from the start. Of course, there's nothing new about stepparenting. Before divorce became widespread, it happened often. When childbirth risks were higher, many mothers died during or after the birth of a child. It was usually expected that the widower would remarry and provide his children with a new mother.

Journaling has proved to be extremely valuable in helping stepparents adjust to coparenting a child. I recommend if you are a stepparent that you read the previous section on adoption, as there are some factors in common, although they may appear different. For instance, in that section, I mentioned the adoption triangle, which consists of (1) adoptive parents, (2) child, and (3) birth parents. The same kind of triangle exists with stepparenting, except that (1) is the stepparent.

Your stepchild's birth parent may be active in the child's life, reside in the same community, and be coparenting or visiting the child on a regular basis. Or the birth parent may be dead, be in another city or country, or have disappeared. In any event, there is always a birth parent in the equation. As a therapist, I can assure you that the birth parent's presence or absence always has a deep influence on a child's life. This cannot be ignored.

When things are *not* going well, stepparenting can be a nightmare. If there is a lot of conflict between the divorced birth parents, or if there is resentment or jealousy on the part of the stepparent or the child's other birth parent, the stress can be intense. An adversarial situation is very painful for everyone, especially the child.

For dealing with the emotions and confusion often associated with stepparenting in general (and this triangle in particular), I recommend the exercise "How I Feel" in the first section of this chapter. Stepparents using this exercise need only replace the word *adoption* with *stepparenting* or any other word that feels appropriate.

Many stepparents tell me that one of the first things they encounter when they free-associate on the word *stepparent* is the
image of the stepmother in "Cinderella." Somehow stepmothers
have gotten a bad rap in fairy tales and fiction. When you do
the free-association part of the exercise, all of that will come
out so you can clear it. If you don't like being referred to as
stepmother or stepfather, perhaps you can find another name
you like and ask the family to refer to you that way. One family
I knew called their stepmother "Mom Two." Others refer to
their stepparent by first name, and when speaking about the
person, they refer to her or him as "Dad's wife" or "Mom's
husband." Be creative.

One thing stepparents must be ready for is the real possibility
that in a moment of anger or rebellion, your stepchild may turn
to you and declare, "You are not my mother [or father]." These
words may sting. *Biologically* it's true, so there's no arguing
with the statement. However, if you are an active coparent, you
are doing everything a parent does to raise and love a child.
Even if the child forgets it, don't *you* ever forget it. If your stepchild ever does say that to you, just remember that all children
sometimes say angry things to their parents, whether they are
adopted, being stepparented, or not. When I was little and got
mad at my mother, I'd cry that I was going to leave home. She
never argued with me. Instead, she'd call my bluff by promptly
going to the closet and getting my suitcase out so that I could
pack it. End of subject. Personally, I prefer Tom Gordon's approach. Just feed back what the child is really saying when she
said, "You can't make me do that. You're not my mother." Instead of reacting all over the place, feeling hurt, or getting angry,
your response might be, "You must be really angry to say something like that." The child will probably agree: "You bet I'm
mad." At this point, you can invite the child to talk about why
she is so mad at you. "Do you want to talk about what's making
you so angry?"

In this way, you disarm the child by accepting her feelings
(which is a way of accepting her). But this takes inner clarity

and emotional neutrality. If you've been doing journal dialogues, you will have had lots of practice with this kind of nonthreatening, nonblaming conversation.

If you find that a child's angry state triggers your own anger,
resentment, or other difficult feelings, I suggest using your journal to explore those feelings. Scribble, draw, and write your feelings in your journal using your *nondominant* hand.

After doing some journal work (perhaps even some journal
dialogues with the child), write a letter. In your journal letter to
the child, share any insights you received about your relationship. You may want to copy the letter out and give it to him or
her. I don't advise being there when the child reads it. The great
thing about letters is that the recipient can just "listen" to what
you have to say without reacting or interrupting. If the child
can't read yet, tape-record your message and let the child play
it for himself or herself.

When there is conflict, another good journal exercise is to
express how you feel about this child and your relationship in
your journal using your *dominant* hand. Just write whatever
comes up.

There may be conflict with your partner at the same time that
problems with the stepchild are brewing. An excellent way to
deal with domestic discord is to use your journal to explore
your relationship with your partner using your *dominant* hand.
Through journaling, a stepmother I knew gained insight into
how to set boundaries and limits with her fifteen-year-old stepson, who had developed a habit of lying in order to get out of
going to school. The boy was faking sore throats and head-
aches, but the stepmother had believed him for awhile. When it
persisted and he refused to go to a doctor, she did some journaling. In writing with her *nondominant* hand, she intuitively
guessed the truth. She also wrote about how yucky it felt to
have been unwittingly covering for him when the school had
called to inquire about his whereabouts. That evening, she sat
father and son down and told them she wouldn't be covering
for the boy anymore. Her husband, who had a habit of abdicating his parental responsibilities and handing them over to others

(first to his ex-wife and now to his current wife), was forced to look at the truth. He could no longer ignore his son's pattern of deception and went in for a parent conference at the school, where counseling was recommended.

Another important aspect of stepparenting, as with all parenting, is the relationship with our Inner Child. Find out how your Inner Child is doing with regard to stepparenting through right-hand/left-hand dialogues like the ones you did in Chapter 3.

Another relationship you can journal about is the one with the child's birth parent, especially if that person is active in parenting the child or if there is any family conflict going on. Try some right-hand/left-hand dialogues: your voice is written with your *dominant* hand, and the other parent's voice speaks with your *nondominant* hand. As always, you can expect some amazing insights with this technique.

BLENDED FAMILIES: THE BRADY BUNCH AND BEYOND

What's a blended family, you ask? It's two adults who both have children from previous marriages or relationships and then come together. They get married or live together, and all the kids get mixed into a new family. So now we have stepparenting in two directions (him with her kids, her with his kids). Then, of course, we have all the relationships between the stepsiblings, not to mention everybody's relationships with ex-spouses ("other parents"). There are usually a bunch of grandparents thrown in there for good measure as well. It can easily become a tribe.

For many years, my father was a leading film editor in television. One of the shows he edited and supervised was about America's favorite blended family, the Brady bunch. On reruns, you can still see Dad's name on the titles: Frank Capacchione. That show went on to become a cult classic. Years later, after having been a single parent, I partnered with a man who had children from a former marriage. When we were in the middle of our own blended domestic scene, I realized how *The Brady Bunch* had prepared my children's generation for this family configuration, which has now become quite commonplace.

Much of what was said earlier in the chapter about adoption and stepparenting applies to blended families. That's why I think it's a good idea for stepparents to read the first two sections of the chapter. However, be warned that blended families are just a *lit-tle* more complicated. Actually, they're a *lot* more complicated.

For instance, the holidays can be a real three-ring circus for blended families. It wasn't quite so bad in our case, because I'm a Christian and he was a Jewish Tibetan Buddhist. We had most of the bases covered in the religion department, and we celebrated all the holidays. There were enough dinners and kids and ex-spouses and grandparents and in-laws to go around, so it seemed to work itself out. I've heard of other cases, however, in which it gets very complicated, and there can be nightmarish games of tug-of-war about where the kids should spend Thanksgiving, Christmas, Hanukkah, or whatever.

Using your journal to explore your feelings, writing letters in your journal, doing right-hand/left-hand dialogues with family members or your Inner Child or wisdom guide can all be great tools for getting through holidays or other events associated with stress.

There are numerous journal exercises elsewhere in this book that will help you deal with blended family situations that have you upset or stumped. I trust that you will discover the ones that are right for you as you go through the book. However, I'd like to suggest a few here:

- *Journal on the topic of "how I feel about this child."* You can do free-associative writing, dialogues, drawings, diagrams, and so on. Be creative. Even if there is more than one stepchild, deal with each individually. Lumping them all together as "his kids" or "her children" can lead to some severe breakdowns in communication. Relate to each of them on separate terms.

- *Another topic is "our blended family."* How do I see the relationship between me and my partner? Between my child and my partner's child? Between my child and my partner? Between me and my partner's child?
- *You can also do collages of the family.* This is a great activity to do together. You can include snapshots, photocopies of pictures from the family album, and drawings. Have fun with this one. My motto is, "The family that plays together stays together."

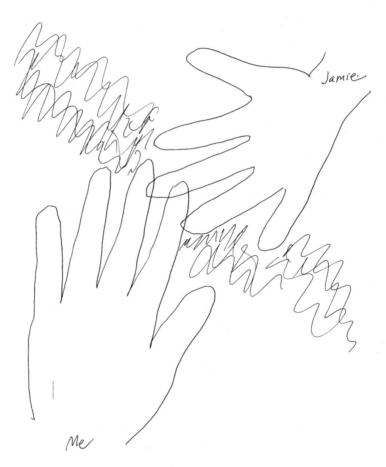

How I feel about Jamie.

I really love Jamie as if she were my own child. I liked her the first time Jim introduced me to her. And I'm sure the feelings are mutual. We just hit it off right away. However, since Jim and I got married and Jamie came to live with us full time (weekends once a month with her natural mom), I've felt some cloudiness at certain times. I don't know any better way to say it than that. Cloudiness, like smog. That's how I pictured it in my drawing: a layer of smog where our finger tips meet.

When Jamie comes home from those visits, she seems unusually quiet and withdrawn for a few hours or even a day. I guess that's understandable. She must miss her Mom, even though she chose to live with us. The problem for me is that I start feeling rejected, the way I did at her age (12), when my Dad was working out of town for a year and we only saw him on weekends. I had a hard time adjusting. I remember reaching out for one more hug before he had to go and feeling somehow abandoned, even though my mother said he was doing it for us.

Maybe I'll tell Jamie what happened to me when I was 12, traveling back and forth to visit Dad in the town where he was working. She might want to talk about how it is for her going back and forth between two households. If I share first, that might open the door for her to talk about it if she wants to. If not, that's O.K. If she needs to be alone with her thoughts and feelings when she comes back from her mom's, I can certainly accept that. The important thing is for us to communicate with each other, like the hands in the drawing, but without the smog.

PART THREE

Parenting
in the School of Life

8

The New Nuclear Family: Two, One, or Many

When it comes to reproduction and forming what we call the basic unit of society, the math has always been simple: one and one make three. According to our laws, religions, media, and customs, we expect a man and a woman to get legally married, then have and raise a baby together. In my generation of people who came of age in the fifties, any other scenario was the exception and was usually whispered about behind closed doors—the pregnant bride, the couple who eloped, the secret abortion, the girl who was sent away to have her baby because the father was too young or had disappeared. If you were an exception, you had broken the rules. You were judged and sometimes ostracized from family or community. Shame and guilt ruled. Divorce was still relatively rare and considered unfortunate, at best.

Obviously things have changed dramatically. The reality is that we have a high divorce rate, pregnancies outside of marriage (especially among teenagers) are common, and many couples who live together and are raising their child remain unmarried. However, in our society, the basic family unit is still officially defined as two parents and a child. In practical terms, both parents are expected to be legally, financially, physically, emotionally, and morally responsible for their offspring. Our society places all decisions regarding health care, religion, child care, education, boundaries and limits on behavior, and so forth squarely in the hands of the natural birth parents (or adoptive parents).

Although babies have always been raised in families and tribes, we need to be aware that the nuclear family—a heterosexual couple and a child (or children) living in their own place—is a recent invention of industrialized nations. The nuclear family represents less than a nanosecond in the history of the human race. Prior to that, families lived in extended family clusters. That was true of our immigrant ancestors and the societies from which they came. Most people on the planet today, especially in nonindustrialized areas, live in some form of extended family culture.

The nuclear family as we know it was actually imprinted into our psyches by TV via family sitcoms like *Ozzie and Harriet, Father Knows Best,* and other shows of the fifties (the pre-civil rights and pre-women's movement days). Perhaps at no time in the history of the human race has "The Family" been so scrutinized, mythologized, caricatured, sentimentalized, lampooned, or revolutionized as it has on television in the last four decades. Why is this so?

One reason is that television, even more so than radio, is the *perfect* medium for looking at the family, both literally and figuratively. It's better than plays, movies, books, or magazines. Television is sitting right there in our homes where we live. We eat, visit, fight, sometimes make love, forge relationships, and even break up in front of the all-seeing eye of the television set. In fact, that all-purpose domestic space called the family room never existed before television. And that's where a lot of TV sets reside. (BTV—before television—there was the parlor, the living room, and then the den.) One of my mentors, the late Buckminster Fuller (inventor of the geodesic dome, futurist, and world citizen who coined the term *spaceship earth*), used to call TV "the third parent." We can't underestimate the influence of television on our attitudes about what a family is (or "should be").

Now back to the fifties for a minute. Along with a very limited definition of family (white, middle-class, nuclear model) being portrayed in fifties sitcoms, topics were also severely limited. For instance, sex was never discussed on family shows. *I Love Lucy* was revolutionary in that Lucy was pregnant with Little Ricky on the show. (Lucille Ball had become pregnant in real life, and the show was threatened with cancellation because showing Lucy in that condition was considered unseemly.) Lucille Ball prevailed, and the rest is history. The show was also a trailblazer in that Lucy's husband, Ricky Ricardo, Sr., was Hispanic. In those days, that was pretty radical. Other than that, during the infancy of this new medium, sitcom parents and kids were white and middle-class. The underlying "message" being broadcast was that this was the model American family.

In a later decade, *The Waltons* (with Grandpa and Grandma in the same house) actually broke new ground with an extended family resembling our European immigrant ancestors (and more recently Hispanic immigrants from Central and South America, as well as immigrants from the Middle East and Asia). Interestingly enough, *The Waltons* was a period piece about the Depression in rural America, and so this legitimized all those family members living under one roof. One can still hear the closing: "Good night, Grandpa; good-night, Grandma. . . . Good night, John-Boy."

In actuality, since the fifties, middle-class white American couples have been expected to have their own households. From the inception of television, mother-in-law jokes were the stock-in-trade of TV stand-up comics, and couples were encouraged to buy a home of their own. The stereotype of the American family in their suburban tract home definitely did not include in-laws living in the same house, although some did. Furthermore, it was easier then to purchase a house. After the Second World War, vets on the G.I. Bill could buy a home with very little or no money down. And whole suburban cities were being built, like the sprawling greater Los Angeles basin. The isolated nuclear family sequestered in the suburbs was as much an economic invention as it was a social one.

Post-World War II America was also a time of growing affluence, and most women went back home (after their war efforts in factories and in the services) and had children. They were the first generation of middle-class women to have the economic luxury of being stay-at-home moms. Their patron saint, Donna Reed, starred in her own family sitcom. This movement of women into the middle- and upper-class world of suburbia was described in Betty Friedan's early sixties book *The Feminine Mystique,* which became required reading for the women's movement.

Divorce was decidedly absent from the picture of the all-American family promulgated by the media in the fifties. Indeed, divorces were much harder to come by in those days. You had to show cause, like adultery, and it took awhile. Divorce was considered the exception.

Influenced by the freedom riders and civil rights movement, women were banding together in consciousness-raising groups, breaking loose from old images, and claiming their civil rights along with minority groups. By 1970, "the women's liberation movement" had been featured in *Time* magazine and covered by other major media. Divorce laws were rewritten, and so was history (sometimes called "*her*story"). The face of the American family was changing dramatically, and so was its image in the media.

In the sixties and seventies, minority groups, working mothers, divorced people, single women and men, the handicapped, and even space aliens (remember *Mork and Mindy?*) began appearing in sitcoms and other television fare. Previously forbidden and impolite topics, like politics and religion and sex, were gradually included. *All in the Family*'s Archie Bunker dared to speak for racists, while his daughter and son-in-law argued their "commie pinko" views (or so said Archie). Topics such as homosexuality began to be included as well. The media were reflecting vastly different attitudes to keep up with reality, and in turn, the media were influencing our reality.

I'm not taking you on this trip down memory lane for nostalgia's sake. Rather, I want to illustrate the fact that three generations have been raised on rapidly changing images of the family on television. Because of reruns, we can see the changes for ourselves. These old images never go away. Like fairy tales, they just keep coming back as retro cult classics (like *The Brady Bunch* feature-length theater release film of the nineties). The shows from my youth are period pieces for "generation X" kids (born in the flower-child sixties). And reruns from the sixties through the eighties look like period pieces to my grandchildren today.

One thing is clear: our definition of the family as portrayed on television and the media is much broader today as a result of four decades of social change. Think about *Sanford and Son, Different Strokes, The Jeffersons, Roseanne,* the controversial *Murphy Brown* (remember Dan Quayle's response to her single-parenting out of wedlock?). And then there's *Ellen.* Although not a "family sitcom" per se, when Ellen dated another lesbian woman (who was a mom) on the show, it entered the arena of family situations.

The point is that if we *thought* we knew what a family was when television first entered American homes in the late forties, we sure don't seem to now. The answer to the question "What is a family?" has so many answers nowadays that it boggles the mind. And yet the *big* questions for you, as a parent, are always going to be: "What is *my* family? Who are *we*? What do my family relationships look like right now?" (Not what you *thought* a family would be, not even what you *wanted* it to be—but what it *is*.)

COUPLES IN PARENTING

If you and a partner (spouse, boyfriend or girlfriend, or "significant other") are parenting a child together, this section is especially for you. If you skipped any chapters in Part II, it would be advisable to read them, even if you don't think you fit some of the categories. There may be some information about parenting there that can be useful for you. If you are not parenting as half of a couple, I'd also recommend that you read this section anyway.

Now let's talk about couples parenting a baby. You've given birth to your child or adopted one. You have welcomed the child into your home and are now engaged in the day-to-day task of caring for him or her. You have had some decisions to make about breast-feeding versus bottle-feeding, about where the baby sleeps and spends his or her waking hours, about who will be with the baby during the day and in the evenings, and so on.

Parenting as partners will present you with many choices to be made together. After awhile, you will shape your own unique style of family life. There are many options, and you need to explore them.

The important thing is to communicate with each other about what your individual needs are, what your relationship needs are, and what is best for your child as well. If you find yourself falling back on stereotypes, comparing yourself to TV families or neighbors or even your own parents, stop and reevaluate what you are doing. The point is to be creative and find the style of parenting that works for you at any given time. Your needs will change, your partner's needs will change, and so will your child's. Be honest and clear about what is really happening. Are you happy about it? If not, how do you want things to be? That's what the next journal exercise will help you do.

Parenting Together

Materials: Journal and felt pens; photo collage materials

Purpose: To become aware of your current needs, your relationship needs, and needs regarding the care of your child

Activity:

1. With your *dominant* hand, write about a typical week in your life right now. Include what you and your partner are doing with your time. Who is responsible for the child? How much time do you spend alone with your partner? With your child? With your child and your partner together? How is that time spent? What do you do together?

2. With your *dominant* hand, continue writing. How has your life changed since welcoming this child into your lives? Do you feel satisfied that the schedule and activities you are currently engaged in are working for you, your partner, and your child? If not, what seems to be the problem for you? Is the child's presence in your lives affecting your relationship with your partner? If so, how? Are there any problems in that area? What about other areas of your life (work, friendships, health, other)? How have they been impacted?

3. Draw a vertical line down your journal page or use two pages side by side. Head the left side "What's Working" and the right side "Needs Change." With your *dominant* hand, fill in each column.

4. With your *nondominant* hand, let your Inner Child write about its needs now that there is a child in your life. How can you meet those needs and still take care of your commitments to your partner and your child?

5. With your *nondominant* hand, write about your biggest concerns regarding your relationship with both your partner and your child at this time. Include such issues as physical and emotional health of the child, your support system, change in lifestyle, work, and impact on your relationship with your partner or other loved ones.

6. Make a collage called "Our Family" using magazine photos, snapshots, or other images. In this collage, include pictures or symbols of your extended family and support system, including other family members, friends, professionals (your baby's pediatrician), baby-sitters, and any other people who are helping you parent your child.

___

After you have done this journal exercise, communicate your insights to your partner so that any problems can be resolved together. Sometimes, it may be a problem only you can solve. Yet you need to share this process with your partner so that he or she understands what's going on for you. In this way, you build intimacy and strengthen your relationship.

CREATIVE PROBLEM SOLVING FOR COUPLES

When you face challenges in your life as a parenting couple, some creative brainstorming can help tremendously. The idea is to open your mind and heart to some truly unique solutions that work for all of you. The tendency is to fall back on the way other people have solved similar problems. You are certainly free to do that if you wish, and if it works. But oftentimes, other people's solutions feel like shoes that don't fit. We try to force ourselves to adapt, but something feels strangely uncomfortable. These are times when we really need to get centered and listen to that "still, small voice within." We need our inner wisdom more than ever, so that we can find the answer that works for us. If we do this, the universe (or Divine Providence or whatever you call it) invariably helps us out.

I'd like to share an example from my own early parenting experience that demonstrates how decisions are made based on deeply held values and goals. When my husband and I had our first child, I wanted to be at home with her. I had already left my full-time job in my sixth month of pregnancy. We both felt good about my staying home during the pre-nursery school years while he worked a full-time job as a college instructor. We could only afford one car, so we sold our two small cars and got a family-worthy VW van.

Although I was staying home with the baby, emotionally and mentally, I needed to stay active as an artist and a teacher. I was able to do freelance design and artwork at home and teach an occasional Saturday class (when my husband could stay home with the baby). In this way, I met my need to continue some professional work, and we met my husband's need to continue his career as well as our financial need for steady income. We could not afford to hire a baby-sitter, nor did we want to. It was important to us that we share the care of our baby between us. The only other people who ever took care of our child were my mother and father, who lived a short commute away. So if we wanted to go out at night or take a short vacation, my parents took the baby for us. Those were our options, and they worked perfectly for us for several years.

By the time our youngest was enrolled in the Montessori pre-school that her older sister was already attending, I was eager to resume a career out of the home. By this time, we had a second car, so I could commute to work. My salary was very good, so we could afford to pay for two Montessori tuitions. We were also very fortunate that at that time, my husband received a research grant and was able to quit his teaching job and work from home. That meant he was available to pick the kids up from school in the afternoon and be with them until I got home at dinnertime.

Some of this was good luck (my parents' being available to baby-sit), but most of it was planning. My husband and I had talked about what we would do when both girls were old enough to be in school. We valued meaningful work and knew we had to honor that commitment to ourselves. I had made my need for a career outside the home known, and he had talked for some time about his desire to do independent research. In fact, we were submitting proposals long before he received the grant. The point is that we each supported the other's individual goals and worked those into our family goals as well. Rather than feeling limited by family duties and responsibilities, we both felt enriched by them. The educational materials and toys we later developed professionally were a direct result of being parents.

Having values and goals as individuals and as a family can strengthen your relationship with your partner and also with your children. If you are building something together, you are forming a working team. The next journal exercise will help you to get clear on where you are going as individuals and as a family and on how you might get there.

Where We're Going

Materials: Journal and felt pens; photo collage materials

Purpose: To become aware of your short- and long-term goals as individuals; to become aware of your relationship goals and family goals

Activity:

1. With your *dominant* hand, write about your personal individual goals in life. Include such things as education, career, health, hobbies, and the like. What kind of support do you want for reaching your goals? From your partner? From others?

2. Still using your *dominant* hand, write about your partner's personal individual goals as you understand them. What is important to your partner? What kind of support can you offer? Share this with your partner to see whether you truly understand his or her personal individual goals. If you're not sure what your partner's goals are, have a meeting and ask him or her to tell you. Then proceed with this exercise.

3. Do you see any obstacles to reaching your goals or your partner's goals? Draw a picture of the goals and the obstacles, using your *nondominant* hand. Then draw a picture of the obstacles being removed.

4. Do a collage showing your individual goals, your partner's goals, and your shared goals as parents. Write about it in your journal with your *dominant* hand.

5. Invite your partner to do a collage with you in which you picture your shared family goals. Do you have a dream house in mind? A desire to move to another city or region or country? What about vacations and play time with each other? With your child? Discuss the collage and put it up where you can both see it. Make additions and revisions as time goes on.

6. In your journal, with your *dominant* hand, write a list based on your shared values and goals as pictured in your collage. Review it from time to time and see how you are doing. Have you taken steps to reach your goals?

In the next journal exercise, you'll be continuing to practice working as a team. This time, your focus will be on solving problems together creatively.

From Challenges to Victories

Materials: Journal and felt pens

Purpose: To become aware of problems that need to be resolved; to find creative solutions

Activity:

1. With your *dominant* hand, write about a current problem you have regarding your relationship with your partner, your child, or family responsibilities in general. How do you feel about this problem?

2. With your *dominant* hand, write a sentence that describes your problem. With your *nondominant* hand, free-associate some solutions. How would you like things to be in relation to this problem? Don't premeditate your answers, and don't try to make sense of your solutions. Just write down whatever comes to mind first. Then sort through what you wrote and see whether your list contains any ideas for practical solutions.

3. Invite your partner to do some brainstorming with you. Together, define the problem, then brainstorm some solutions without judging them. Write them all down, both of you using your *nondominant* hand. Then go through the solutions and pick one you can live with. If that one doesn't work, try the process again.

WHEN THERE IS CONFLICT

If conflicts arise between you and your partner, or if communication seems to be breaking down, I would suggest that you do a journal dialogue. Write out an imaginary conversation with your partner using both hands. This is for you and you alone. Your voice will be written with your *dominant* hand, and your partner's voice will be written with your *nondominant* hand. This exercise can help you make the spiritual connection with your partner's higher self. It may also give you some much-needed insights into what's going on between you, what you are projecting on your partner, and how you really feel about the situation.

You can also write a journal letter to your partner. If you feel you want to share it with your partner later, you can copy it out and give it to him or her. Or you can read it aloud when the two of you have reserved a time and place to be together without interruptions. This can help tremendously in opening lines of communication and rebuilding intimacy between the two of you.

Writing a love letter to your partner on a fairly regular basis can also strengthen the bond between you. Mutual love letter writing can be extremely valuable, whether communications are breaking down or not. Such letters tend to support the shared experiences you have and reaffirm your commitment to each other.

PARENTING ON YOUR OWN

If you are a single parent, this section is intended for you. Many parents are raising children alone these days. The divorce rate coupled with the increase in teen pregnancies outside of marriage have made single-parenting so common that we no longer think of it as the exception. It has simply become another way of raising children.

Having "been there and done that" myself, my best advice to single parents is this: establish a strong support system, especially if your child (or children) live with you most or all of the time. Whether there is another parent involved who provides financial support, visitations, or a place for your child to live or whether your child's other parent is absent from the scene altogether, getting help from others will be crucial for your and your child's mental and emotional health. To be totally responsible for a child is a huge task for an individual to bear. Be creative in building the support team that you want. Look for acceptance of who you are, respect, moral support, and encouragement. The principle of nonjudgment is very important here. Avoid people who criticize or tell you how to parent your child. Seek out those who can acknowledge the hard work involved in single-parenting and offer help in some way when you need it. Be sure the relationships with your support team are mutual. You need to reciprocate in whatever way you can.

When I was first adapting to the job of single-parenting, I cultivated a few new friendships that became very close. These people helped me tremendously. When I got sick, they car-pooled my children to school. When my car broke down, they gave me a ride to the mechanic's shop and provided transportation for errands, and so on and so forth. It's all those little daily dilemmas that can really get to you when you are the one adult in the household who is responsible for everything. My friends taught me how to reach out for help by loving me and offering assistance when I needed it. I learned about friendship, about acceptance and true caring, when I was most vulnerable. They showed me what a support system really is and helped me to see the value of the extended-family-by-choice.

If you are just beginning single-parenting, it would be good to revisit the exercise entitled "My Support Team" in Chapter 4. Of course, there are many exercises in Chapters 1 through 4 that will help you deal with the changes you'll face in becoming a single parent.

Chapter 3, "The Inner Family," is an extremely important one for single parents. Knowing how to nurture yourself is such an important survival tool for single parents that I think Inner Family work should be done on an ongoing basis. In fact, it was during the days when I was parenting my children alone that I discovered Inner Family work. Without it, I don't know what I would have done.

Chapter 4 has many exercises that can help you maintain balance and stay centered when confronted with the many challenges and responsibilities you face as a single parent.

Above all, avoid isolating yourself. Reach out and ask for help. It's not always easy, and sometimes you may get "no" for an answer, but if you don't try, you'll never find out. I also recommend counseling or a support group. If you can't afford a therapist, investigate community agencies, organizations like Parents Without Partners, church-sponsored counseling programs, or clinics that offer a sliding-scale fee.

I highly recommend free support groups for single parents. Find an organization or informal support group or form one of your own. When I was studying Parent Effectiveness Training, a group called MOMMA was formed that provided strong emotional support, networking, and information for single parents. I even taught a P.E.T. course to this group. It was a fantastic experience, and I received as much as I gave through teaching the course. As a single parent, I was able to hear how others were dealing with the same challenges I was facing.

There are also some journal exercises for couples in the previous section of this chapter that can be valuable for single parents. Values clarification and problem-solving exercises can help you to open your mind and heart to a range of options you might not have considered before. It just takes some time and inner reflection. The answers are all there inside.

PARENTING IN AN EXTENDED FAMILY

Some of you reading this book may be parenting a child (or children) on your own and could technically be defined as single parents. Yet you might actually be living in an extended family situation. I've known single parents who shared a house with another family or another single parent. I've also known single parents living with relatives (parents, siblings, uncles or aunts, and so forth) who shared some of the parenting responsibilities with them. When I worked in Head Start, many of our inner-city single moms lived with their own mothers and younger siblings. This enabled the mother with young children to go to work and the grandmother to stay home and provide child care.

If you are living in an extended family with blood relations or an extended-family-by-choice, the exercises presented earlier in this chapter can be just as valuable for you. Your relationships with extended family members can be explored in your journal. Interpersonal problems can often be solved using techniques provided in the section for couples. And there are journal activities in Chapter 7 that can help you sort out the many relationships you have, especially if you are sharing a house with another single parent and are dealing with his or her children. It is very much like a blended family, even though you may not be in an intimate relationship with your adult housemate. For that reason, I recommend that you read the exercises for blended families and use the ones that seem most relevant for you.

CHILD CARE AND BABY-SITTING

Sooner or later, all parents have to deal with the issue of child care, baby-sitting, or live-in care. Whether you are parenting with a partner, raising a child on your own, or living in an extended family situation, there will be times when you will have to make a decision about entrusting your child to the care of others. Anyone who is taking care of your child becomes part of your extended family, if only for an evening of baby-sitting. This person is an integral member of your support team.

There are many categories of people who provide child care, both professional and amateur. Some are paid, experienced professionals who come into homes for extended periods or actually live with the family by trading room and board for part of their salary. We used to call these people nannies; now they are called *au pairs*. Nonprofessional baby-sitters who come in for an evening or a day are often high school students but may be older people as well. Many of my friends who don't have grandparents living in the same city seek out older women who have had children of their own and are available to help out from time to time for a nominal fee. As one friend told me, "My kids need that grandma energy around. They love it."

For working parents who need full-time child care, there are several choices. There is child care in your own home. This can be live-in child care, in which the au pair lives with you full-time. There is also child care during daytime working hours only, in which the baby-sitter comes to your home each day.

There are also infant and day care centers in a range of sizes. Some of these child care services are offered in private homes by people who are licensed to care for infants, toddlers, and young children. Others are commercially owned businesses in a day care center for larger groups of infants and children operated by a staff of workers. Another option used by some working parents is the trusted neighbor who will take the child into her home during the day for a reasonable fee. Another possibility in some communities is the corporation-sponsored child care center for the employees' preschool children.

Which form of child care you select will depend on what is available, the quality of care, the trustworthiness of the child care provider, cost, schedule, accessibility, and appropriateness for your particular child's needs.

With respect to the long-term impact on your child, choosing child care is an extremely important decision. The character and professional competence of the people to whom you entrust your child should be a top priority. There have been many stories in the media in recent years about molestation, abuse, and neglect in child care situations. Whether it revolves around a nursery school (as in the famous McMartin Preschool case) or involves a nanny (as with the more recent case of the British au pair whose charge actually died), these stories have alerted parents to the need for extreme caution.

There are many referral sources to which you can turn for recommendations: your friends and neighbors; your pediatrician, childbirth educator, or other health care professional; local women's organizations such as La Leche League (which provides support for breast-feeding); your church or temple; or your employer's human resources department (if you work for a large company).

You can approach this decision the same way you did health care during pregnancy and your birth plan. Use your journal to identify what you want and then set about finding it. Here's a journal exercise to help you in setting priorities for child care and developing questions to be asked at the interview with any potential provider of child care services for your family.

Care for My Child

Materials: Journal and felt pens

Purpose: To become aware of your current needs regarding child care; to find the best care for your child at this time

Activity:

1. With your *dominant* hand, write about your child care needs at this time. What kind of child care do you need? What hours? What kind of services do you want for your child? What particular or special needs does your child have? How much can you afford to pay? Any other concerns?

2. With your *nondominant* hand, draw a picture of the ideal child care situation for your child. Who is your child with? What is that person (or staff) like? How does that person (or staff) treat your child? What is your child doing in this child care situation? How does your child feel? You can use cartoon speech bubbles next to the child care worker and your child to express what they say or how they feel.

3. With your *dominant* hand, write down how you can go about finding the kind of care you want for your child. What are your local resources and sources of referrals?

4. Write out a list of topics for an interview. Include the following topics if the provider of extended child care will be working in your home:
   - Prior experience
   - Education or credentials, legal status
   - Criminal record (can be checked through city or county agencies)
   - Long-term goals (How long will she be able to work for you?)
   - Philosophy about child rearing
   - Examples of emergencies or problems she's solved in the past
   - Three referrals from former employers
   - Smoking, drinking
   - Transportation (to and from your home)
   - Fees, schedule, and availability
   - Scope of work (feeding, bathing, walks, and so forth)
   Include the following topics if the provider is a child care director at a center or in a private home:
   - Licenses, credentials of staff, insurance coverage
   - Training and educational background of staff, CPR skills, and so on

- Criminal records screening of director and staff
- Experience of staff, how long the center has been in business
- Referrals from other parents using the center
- Fee schedule and vacation or missed-day policies

5. After the interview (at which your child should be present), use your journal to explore your reaction and that of your child. Write with your *dominant* hand. Then ask for your Inner Child's reaction. As usual, ask questions with your *dominant* hand; let the Inner Child answer with your *nondominant* hand.

If you're hiring a nanny or au pair to work in your home, you need to be clear about your ground rules, such as no personal visitors while your child is being cared for, no smoking, drinking. Obviously you want a person who does not take drugs, and that will be established in the interview. It's a good idea to be there for part of the first day. Be in the house, but let her do the work. You can show her where everything is, see how she and your child relate to each other, and get a sense about her in the real situation.

After the first days in child care, you'll be able to tell whether your child is happy and contented in the situation. Observe the quality of interaction between your child and the care provider every chance you get. If you ever feel that something is wrong, check it out immediately. It's too important to procrastinate about. The next chapter will provide you with journal exercises that focus on developing greater awareness of your child through observation. Using your journal to process your observations will make you more sensitive and responsive to your child's needs.

Remember that your child's relationship with a nanny, au pair, or day care provider will be the beginning of a socialization process that eventually extends to the community of school, clubs, special classes, church or temple, and so forth. There will probably be some separation anxiety at first. It's normal for a child to fuss and cry when parents leave him with people he doesn't know. If the situation is a healthy one, in time he will grow to feel comfortable with the care provider. If not, then you'll need to repeat the process of research until you and your child are satisfied. Be patient, but be persistent. Settle only for the best.

9

Growing with Your Child

BUILDING A FOUNDATION

The first few days of a baby's life can bring a deeply spiritual opening between parent and child. The sheer mystery of birth and the vulnerability of this tiny being you hold in your arms are truly awe-inspiring. Many mothers and fathers have told me that they had no way to predict the powerful emotions that poured forth during those first days of parenting. Tears of joy, moments of awed silence, feelings of being honored but also humbled by the huge task that lay ahead—all following in rapid succession. In some cultures, the time immediately following birth is sacred and protected for both mother and child. Relieved of other tasks and allowed to simply *be a mother,* she devotes herself to nothing but her newborn.

In our hectic society, the dramatic transition of birth calls for rest and recovery for parents and child alike. There are many adjustments to make—lifestyle, schedule, sleep patterns, and so forth—and there is much to do. This is when your support system will be invaluable, helping with meals, errands, household chores, and more.

For the baby, the first days of life are about getting to know a foreign world of lights and sights, people and moving objects, new sounds and textures. Your baby's sense of touch is one of her chief ways of gathering information, especially about people. She is highly sensitive to the quality of human interaction communicated through cradling, holding, massage, and other gentle and reassuring touch. Research shows that babies deprived of physical contact become listless and ill, and in extreme cases, may even die. Babies who are handled carelessly or abrasively are also affected and may become chronically fussy or withdrawn. Loving physical contact counts for a great deal with babies.

Your baby can see at close range, can follow moving objects, and especially enjoys looking at faces. He can hear (as he did in utero), and recognizes your voice. His sense of smell allows him to detect the scent of your body. His taste buds are well developed, and he can distinguish differences in tastes. All of this means that your baby comes ready to relate to you. And indeed, the first few weeks of parenting are a time for creating the foundation of your relationship with your child.

There are some general stages of infant and child development that you will learn about simply from observing and interacting with your child. Gathering information from books, videos, and classes can help you understand these stages of growth (see the bibliography). However, there is nothing quite like direct observation. As you cultivate awareness of this unique being who has been entrusted to your care, a special bond will begin forming. You will be establishing a kind of rapport that is characteristic of the parent-child relationship. As you become sensitive to the unique cries, grunts, smiles, sighs, laughs, body language, and facial expressions of your baby, a personality will become evident to you. As in any relationship, this takes time and is built upon shared experience.

Although it may seem as if you are doing all the giving (especially when the baby is very small), what you are receiving from your child is an opportunity that cannot be measured. You are being given a chance to really learn what it means to love and cherish and nurture another human being. What you do for your child, you are also doing for yourself. What you do *to* your child, you also do to yourself. Good parenting is all about the golden rule.

Accepting your baby as she is, rather than wanting her to be something else, will help the relationship get off to a good start. Whether you have acquired a lot of information about infant behavior or not, it is your willingness to get to know your baby and her unique ways of being that will be most important.

Accepting *yourself* as you are, rather than trying to be something else, will help you accept your child. Being totally honest with yourself (as you have in earlier chapters) about how you feel, what you need, and how to get your needs met will go a long way toward enabling you to meet your child's needs with generosity of spirit. In doing the journal activities in this book, you have been learning to understand and accept yourself and your partner. Now you will be using the same tools for learning to understand and accept this very special being who is your child.

Baby and Me

Materials: Journal and felt pens

Purpose: To become aware of your feelings about having a baby and about caring for your baby

Activity:
  1. With your *nondominant* hand, draw a picture of you and your baby.
  2. With your *nondominant* hand, write down your feelings about the baby and about being the parent of this child.
  3. With your *dominant* hand, write down any concerns or problems you have regarding your parenting role. Read over what you wrote and review your resources for helping with these concerns or problems. Consider your support system and who might be able to assist you if you need help.
  4. With your *dominant* hand, write a love letter to your baby.

5. Write a dialogue with your baby. Write your own voice with your *dominant* hand and the baby's voice with your *nondominant* hand.
6. With your *dominant* hand, write a prayer of thanks to the Creator for the gift of this child in your life.

————————

Children speak a different language than adults do. We rely heavily on spoken words, whereas babies communicate their needs in sounds, gestures, facial expression, body movements, and moods. Dependent on words as we are, it can sometimes be frustrating when a baby is fussing and we can't figure out what the problem is. There are no simple answers to such questions as "Why is the baby crying?" Different cries signify different things, and with time, attention, and experience, a parent learns the language of the young child.

The next journal exercise is for recording your observations of your baby's behavior and growth. As you do, you will detect his unique personality emerging. Using all your senses, you'll be getting to know your child and developing your capacity for attentiveness to his needs. This exercise can be done repeatedly throughout the first couple of years and will help you understand all the varieties of nonverbal communication that infants and toddlers use constantly.

Getting to Know You

Materials: Journal and felt pens

Purpose: To become aware of your baby's development and needs; to cultivate communication with your baby

Activity:

1. With your *dominant* hand, write down any observations of your baby. Include anything that has caught your attention—movement, facial expressions, sounds, crying, sleep patterns, waking activity, symptoms (such as colic or rashes). Specifically, what signals do you recognize as your

child communicating his needs? How do you meet your baby's needs? What behavior seems to indicate wet diapers or hunger? How does your baby indicate a need for contact, holding or play, or simply a change of scenery?

2. Have you noticed any new skills that the baby has developed? Describe them using your *dominant* hand. Be sure to include the baby's age in weeks or months. Draw a time line horizontally across the next journal page. Below the line, write in the date. Above the line, write in the new skills your child has acquired.

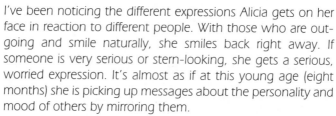

I've been noticing the different expressions Alicia gets on her face in reaction to different people. With those who are outgoing and smile naturally, she smiles back right away. If someone is very serious or stern-looking, she gets a serious, worried expression. It's almost as if at this young age (eight months) she is picking up messages about the personality and mood of others by mirroring them.

She really reacts strongly to certain behaviors, too. She gets very upset if people are yelling at each other or expressing anger. Like the two boys who were fighting in front of the supermarket last week. Alicia immediately started fussing and reached out to me from her shopping cart seat, wanting me to pick her up (which I did). She seemed to want my protection from the boys' angry outburst.

I can also tell the difference between that kind of gesture and the way she tells me (nonverbally) that she has dirty diapers. She gets an annoyed look on her face, kicks her legs or, if she's sitting, she bounces up and down. It's as if she's trying to get out of her diapers. When it comes to hunger, she starts sucking on her fingers and whimpering. And we finally figured out the sign that she needs sleep. Alicia whines like a siren. Give her a stuffed animal at those times, and she's out in two minutes. But it took quite a while to figure out what the whine meant. Probably when we've decoded all her nonverbal messages, she'll start talking.

As you observe your child, it is equally important to observe your own reactions to her behavior, her needs, and your ability to meet those needs. In the early days of parenting, it is perfectly natural to feel some lack of self-confidence, fatigue, and sometimes even resentment. Taking care of a baby is a huge responsibility. Just because a baby is adorable and you are happy to have this child in your life doesn't mean that you don't have a whole range of emotional responses to your role as parent. Journaling can help in exploring those many feelings, accepting them, and expressing them in a safe place. Journaling can also help you expand your repertoire of ways to comfort your child or play with her—in other words, to spend quality time together.

Time Together

Materials: Journal and felt pens; photo collage materials

Purpose: To become aware of your response to your baby; to revisit your values and concerns about parenting at this time

Activity:

1. Think about how you are caring for your baby. Consider things such as health care, baby-sitting, and time you spend with the baby. Draw a vertical line down your journal page or use two pages side by side. Head the left side "What's Working" and the right side "Needs Change." With your *dominant* hand, fill in each column.

2. Sometimes, feelings of inadequacy come up in spite of all we're doing for our child. For instance, when you've investigated all other causes of crying or fussiness, do you find that your baby may just need to cry and to feel safe doing that? Do you feel powerless or frustrated at those times? Irritated or resentful? Can you be with your baby and cuddle him during those times? What feelings come up for you? Write about those feelings with your *dominant* hand.

3. Draw a series of cartoon pictures with your *nondominant* hand showing you and your baby spending quality time together. What do you do to comfort your baby and to play with her? Do you comfort your baby by cuddling, gentle rocking (perhaps in a rocking chair), rubbing her tummy, holding her in your lap, feeding her (when she's hungry), changing soiled clothes, singing or humming to her, talking to her in a loving voice or playing lullabies or soothing music, wrapping her in warm clothes when it's cold, cooling her off when it's hot, taking her for a drive in the car? Playing with your baby might include gently massaging his feet, playing peekaboo, dancing and swaying to music with him in your arms, playing with brightly colored toys or with water in the bathtub, taking him for a walk around the house or the neighborhood. Picture these little scenes in your journal.

4. From time to time, make a new collage called "Our Family," using magazine photos, snapshots, or other images. Incorporate into this collage, pictures or symbols of your extended family and support system, including other family members, friends, professionals (your baby's pediatrician), baby-sitters, and any other people who are helping you parent your child. You may want to do these collages in a scrapbook or photo album.

As you expand your support system, you will be using the services of professionals, such as pediatricians. In selecting professional care, you can use step 1 of the "Health Care, Me, and My Baby" exercise in Chapter 5. Substitute the word *pediatric* for *prenatal* and focus on getting the best care for your child. As with prenatal care, you want to be sure that your child's emotional as well as physical needs are being met in whatever medical care he receives. Be sure also that you feel listened to and respected as his parent.

BUILDING TRUST AND SAFETY

As you spend quality time with your baby learning to communicate with each other, you are creating a bond of safety and trust.

Your baby needs this in order to prepare for the next stages of growth, which will move him from complete dependence on you to a desire to explore the world on his own. These early months of repeated interactions and relating in a caring and attentive manner are paving the way for a time when your child will sit up for himself, begin crawling and exploring his world, then standing, and eventually walking and talking. If you have fully accepted the infant as the dependent being he is in the early months, you have responded according to the child's needs and developmental level. Parents who do this are more likely to grow with their child into the next phase as he literally takes the first steps toward separation and independence. And it doesn't take that long; it's only a matter of several months.

However, at this juncture (and all other transitions to new levels of needs and skills), it is extremely important not to impose external performance standards on your child. Being aware of normal stages of growth and development is one thing, but making comparisons or trying to keep up with the Joneses' kids will weaken your relationship with your child. No child likes feeling that she is not OK the way she is but would be lovable "if only" she measured up to some *ideal* or expectation devised by others. (In fact, no adult likes to feel that way either. In this respect, all humans are the same, regardless of their age.)

Just remember the golden rule. Don't do to your child what you would not want done to you. I know it's easier said than done, for there is a great temptation to use children as "proof" that we are good parents (especially if we feel insecure in the role). How do we try to prove ourselves as parents? By trying to control the child, showing him off in front of others, or comparing him to other kids and looking for ways in which he is ahead of his mates. Being genuinely happy about your child's steps of growth is healthy and normal. But using your child to prove you are a good parent gets you and your child into a tug-of-war, a battle of wills. Nobody wants to live in a battle zone, so be aware of that fine line between setting limits and being a control freak.

In summary, the first year of life, your baby learns about self-esteem from how you treat her. Your job is to welcome this baby into the world. Give her a place in your home and in your life. Accept and appreciate her for who she is, a unique being with her own rhythms, perceptions, abilities, talents, personality traits, and so on. Know in your heart that she is lovable and capable. Love her unconditionally, no matter where or when, even in the middle of the night when she's kept you awake for hours. That's not to say that you won't be exhausted and feel cranky at such times. But what you *do* about it is your choice. You can take it out on your child (or partner or anyone else around), or you can reflect upon your feelings and your behavior and choose what to do about them.

Fortunately, you have the Creative Journal tools for handling that challenge and have been using them in previous chapters. *I cannot repeat too often the need to revisit earlier exercises, especially the ones having to do with self-nurturing, Inner Family work, and creating harmony within yourself and your home (Chapters 2 through 4).*

Caring for an infant brings up all kinds of self-esteem issues for parents: Am I capable of being a good parent? What about my feelings of irritation, frustration, resentment, fatigue? Do they mean I'm a bad parent? It also brings up the importance of knowing your own needs and being responsible for getting them met. In other words, you need to grow up and be fully responsible for yourself and your own happiness in order to raise a child. If you weren't taking good care of yourself before welcoming a child into your life, now is the time to do so. That's why I called this chapter "Growing with Your Child." Nothing matures people as much as parenting.

EXPLORATION AND FREEDOM

If you've treated your infant with love and respect, and have taken good care of yourself as well, the next stage of your child's growing independence will feel like a natural step. That's because it is. Later in the baby's first year, when he sits up and crawls around on his own, it will be obvious that he is growing into a curious, active creature who is eager to explore the world through all of his senses. He goes through what Montessori called "periods of sensitivity" in which certain skills are more naturally developed because of an inherent instinct on the child's part. Learning through touching everything is typical of this period. The child manipulates anything he can get his hands on and often puts things in his mouth. Why? Because an infant's sucking mechanism is highly developed. It has been his link to the world (through breast-feeding or bottle-feeding for sustenance and comfort). It is a way for him to gather information and gain control.

During this period, your child will acquire many new skills and do so more rapidly than at any other time in her life. She is a little sponge, soaking up experience with a great instinct-driven hunger. Trying to block this natural desire to reach out, to experiment, and to take the world in will only frustrate you and your child. This is a good time to reevaluate your home environment and create spaces where your child can be safe in this normal and necessary phase of exploration. This is a time when the child is developing coordination and control, but these skills must be mastered by interacting with a variety of objects, materials, textures, and moving parts as well as people. Child-proofing the areas where your child spends most of her time will protect her, the environment, and your nerves. Creating a situation in which you are constantly saying, "No, don't touch!" or having to rescue your child from breakable or sharp objects is stressful for you and the child.

On the plus side, there are many simple household objects that can be used for stimulating your child's natural curiosity and need to manipulate things. There are pots and pans, nesting plastic or metal measuring cups or bowls, and so forth. There are also any number of self-teaching toys on the market for teaching size and shape discrimination. Materials that can be manipulated by small hands, nested, fit into sockets, and matched for shape, size, and color are highly appropriate. Activities for practicing eye-hand coordination and muscle control are valuable at this stage of development.

If you create a child-friendly place in your home—such as your child's room, den, or family room—it will be easier to allow your child free play among objects that help develop his curiosity and desire to learn. Just be careful not to overdo it. Many parents overstimulate their youngsters with too much stuff. In this case, less is probably better. You can rotate the toys and other objects, displaying a limited number at any given time. Some of the exercises in Chapter 4 will help you reassess the appropriateness of the arrangements in your home. You'll need to stay current based on each stage of development as your child grows and his needs change. For instance, a child's room that works for a two-year-old will no longer be adequate for a seven-year-old.

THE FINE ART OF LIMITS AND BOUNDARIES

In creating limits and boundaries (for the sake of your child's safety and your own sanity), journaling is an excellent way to establish your values and get clear on everyone's needs. Chapters 1 and 2 as well as 4 can help you reconsider your expectations and rules. After all, you are living in a family setting. Everything cannot revolve around your child. As she gets older, she will need to learn about rules, limits, and boundaries. For example, certain *places* may be off-limits to the child, like mom's home office or dad's garage workshop filled with potentially dangerous power tools. A latch on the door will help in the beginning, but as the child understands the word *no*, it will be appropriate to communicate what areas are off-limits.

Some *behaviors* will also be unacceptable, like running across the street without holding an adult's hand. Expectations need to be communicated clearly and reinforced with consistency. With the nonverbal child, who can't understand reasoning, simply picking him up when he runs toward the street will say more than a hundred words. Or the simple word *no* will communicate more than a string of sentences that are incomprehensible to the child.

Doing some journaling about your ground rules, limits, and boundaries regarding off-limits places and behaviors is a valuable way to clarify your expectations. If you are clear, your child will be, too. The point is to create safe and clear boundaries providing security for your child, enabling him to grow and flourish as a curious, independent being.

Explorations and Boundaries

Materials: Journal and felt pens

Purpose: To become aware of your child's growing need for independence and safe boundaries; to clarify your values and ground rules

Activity:

1. With your *dominant* hand, write about your child's current level of interests and skills. What does she gravitate toward? What does she most enjoy doing? Are there any conflicts between your child's natural tendencies and your family's needs? Write about them. What do you do when there is a conflict?

2. With your *dominant* hand, write about your ground rules, spoken and unspoken. What behaviors are unacceptable to you? What do you do when your child engages in one of these behaviors? Are you satisfied with the results? If not, what can you do to change the situation? Write about it, then with your *nondominant* hand, draw a picture of the way you'd like it to be.

   Note: If you share parenting with a partner or an extended family, share your ground rules with them. See whether there are any differences between or among you regarding expectations, boundaries, limits, and the like with respect to your child's behavior.

As limits are put firmly in place, expect your child to test them. That's how she finds out who she is and who's in charge. Be clear about this because it's easy to go to the extreme in either direction: you become a controlling tyrant or a wimpy doormat. There's a middle ground in which you respect your child, but you also respect yourself as the adult who's responsible for establishing and maintaining the ground rules. Your child needs these rules in order to prepare for socialization in the world in a later stage of development. *You* need ground rules in order to maintain your sanity and self-respect as an adult. Permissivism is as detrimental for children as it is annoying for adults.

When the 2 older boys rough-house in the back seat while I'm driving. It really makes it hard to drive safely! I'll pull to the side and stop until THEY STOP. And tell them why I'm stopping.

How I'd like it to be. Safe + NON-HECTIC

Patience is a virtue you'll have lots of opportunities to cultivate during this stage of your child's development. In years to come, you'll remember these days (which include the temper tantrums of the "terrible twos"), especially when your child becomes a teenager. For toddlers and adolescents have a lot in common. They're leaving their dependent stage and moving toward greater independence. Teens are simply doing it at a higher octave (or lower, if you consider voice changes during puberty).

Due to the dramatic nature of these transitions from dependence to budding independence, emotions often run high (for the child as well as the parents). That's when your habit of using your journal to explore your feelings will prove to be a real ally. The point is that you need to release pent-up emotions in a safe way so that you can make it safe for your child to express his feelings safely. Accepting your child's emotions (as you have accepted yours in your journal) is a wonderful way to communicate to your child that you love him no matter what he feels. "There are no bad feelings," you are saying to the child. "They're all OK. You can express them safely here." I recommend designating a special place and materials for your child to vent feelings. Select materials that are appropriate to your child's age and level of coordination, starting with Play-Doh and clay.

As your child matures, materials such as crayons and paper, finger paint, tempera and brushes, and other art supplies can be provided in a place set aside for such activities. Obviously you need to supervise this in the beginning. As your child grows and begins to draw, read, and write, you can introduce him to *The Creative Journal for Children* (Shambhala Publications). This is a wonderful way to foster literacy and academic skills while providing a means for emotional expression. The youngest child (age five or so) can begin with drawing in his journal. As he learns to write the alphabet, on 3″ × 5″ cards, you can write out feeling words that he requests. One five-year-old, who had his own journal, drew a picture of being angry at his brother. He showed the drawing to his mother and told her it was a picture of "mad." His mom, a veteran journal-keeper, asked her son if he'd like to write the word. The boy was learning to write in preschool and had expressed enthusiasm about his newfound skill. His mom printed the letters *M A D* on a card and handed it to her son. The boy printed the word onto the bottom of his journal drawing. From that day forward, his interest in letters and in writing skyrocketed, and his preschool teacher commented on it at their next parent conference.

Movement and dance, singing, and music are also excellent forms of emotional expression for children, as are drama and mime. In a federally funded elementary school research project that I directed, we used arts to teach basic skills. Reading and math scores went up as much as 20 percentile points in one year. The arts can be both psychologically therapeutic and educationally beneficial at the same time. They are even used for healing purposes in hospitals and groups for children with life-threatening or chronic illness or for those who are undergoing surgery or convalescence.

Your child may be taking music or dance or art lessons, but be sure that it isn't *all* performance-oriented. Reserve some form of art expression as a means for your child to release feelings. In this case, the *process* is more important than the product.

THE BALANCE BETWEEN DEPENDENCE AND INDEPENDENCE

Child rearing is a constant balancing act. As long as your child is in his formative years, there will be movement back and forth from dependence to independence and back again. Knowing when to pull in the reins and when to loosen up is a fine art that parents learn over time. Showing your preschooler how to tie his own shoelaces and teaching your sixteen-year-old to drive a car are not so dissimilar in the long run. Both skills are preparing him for more freedom (and responsibility). The same theme will repeat itself throughout your years of parenting, even after your son or daughter leaves home.

Watching your child grow into a separate being with her own thoughts, feelings, and experiences will present you with great challenges and many moments of exhilaration. The crises that every child faces from time to time—the broken arm, the childhood illnesses, the problems at school, and all the other typical dues that children pay on the way to growing up—are tests for the parents as well. These are times when it is clear that your child is utterly dependent on you.

Later the challenges revolve around his burgeoning independence. Whether your four-year-old is leading a separate life in nursery school, your nine-year-old is surpassing you on the computer, or your fourteen-year-old is discovering the opposite sex, the dynamic is the same. The child whom you thought belonged to you shows you—in no uncertain terms—that he has a life of his own. Honest and open communication, respect for who your child is and what he is dealing with, and faith in the process of growth will be important virtues to foster in yourself.

On the other hand, the pride you'll feel in your child's accomplishments, and in watching her learn from her mistakes and mature in the process, are some of the peak experiences of parenting. As I said at the beginning of this book, there are no guarantees that things will turn out the way you'd expected or planned. Your child is her own person. Never forget that. However, if you are committed to developing a deeper understanding of and appreciation for this being who is in your care, you and the child cannot help but benefit from the effort.

It has been my experience that the Creative Journal can be a treasured companion on the path of parenting, a friend indeed when you are in need. I trust you will find your way to the exercise that fits for you at any given time. In the pages of your journal, you can express your feelings, reflect on your thoughts and beliefs, clarify your values, and celebrate those sweet moments when your child says or does something that touches you deeply, right down to your heart and soul. At other times, our children can break our hearts. But then we can pray, as one fifteen-year-old girl did in her journal. After experiencing a broken heart, she drew a heart with a hole in it and then wrote, "Well, whatever God gives me is right, so may my heart be open." Her wounded heart became an open one.

PARENTING THE SPECIAL NEEDS CHILD

Children who are physically, emotionally, or mentally challenged are called "special children." I have found that their parents are very special, too. They face some incredible tests right along with their children. Although they do the same parental dance of balancing between their child's dependence and independence, these parents have to deal with far more complex issues. For instance, their child may look or behave quite differently from other children. This difference is often perceived by others in society as a liability and a reason to exclude or in some way distance themselves from the child.

Also, less is expected of such children even when it isn't necessary. For instance, years ago in a television interview, Stevie Wonder was asked how he felt about being blind as a kid. This consummate artist spoke about how his mother had treated him in childhood. His mother never made him think he was different or odd because he was blind. He showed talent in music and she just expected him to develop it. That's what he wanted and that's what she wanted. He never felt less than anybody else, because his mother never saw him that way.

It would be easy for parents of a child who is challenged in this way to feel cheated, angry, sad, resentful, bitter, and all the rest of it because the child is not like other children. The point is that every child is special, every child is unique, and keeping that in mind is of the utmost importance no matter who your child is or what obstacles he faces in life. Granted, some parents whose children face more challenges than most will be tested and tested and tested again. Special schools, tutors, tests, treatments, surgery, medical interventions, and so forth can be expensive, tedious, and especially difficult if the child is in physical or emotional pain.

Some of my good friends have raised children who were mentally retarded, blind, deaf, had Down's syndrome, severe learning disabilities, psychological disorders, cancer, and numerous other conditions. I am always amazed at the strength and determination these parents and their children have developed over the years. And the talent that has surfaced has been immense.

One couple living in my community, the Farrars, have a son, Jason, who is blind. His musical talent is immense. In his early twenties, this accomplished keyboard artist and bandleader is studying at our local college, performs in clubs and concerts, and also composes music. His parents have always been committed to providing Jason with everything he needs to bring out his best, often at great personal sacrifice.

Raising a special child requires that parents focus on what the child has and is, not on what she lacks. I believe this is a good lesson for all of us. When I hear people complaining that they don't have time to cultivate this talent or that ability, I think of Jason. Neither he nor his parents indulged in excuses, and as a result, he is an accomplished performing artist. Whether the special child ever performs or attains anything in the outer world is beside the point. What is important is that the child be accepted for who she is and given every opportunity to find her personal best. But that is true for all children.

One of the most difficult aspects of parenting a special child is dealing with other people's feelings, such as sympathy, discomfort, patronizing attitudes, judgment, and so on. The sight of a handicapped or challenged child can bring up lots of emotions in family members, friends, neighbors, and strangers passing by. Other children can be very cruel and even may ridicule the child. Many people (old and young alike) can be extremely insensitive in casual comments or furtive looks that they think the special child does not notice. Even if the child cannot notice, the parent usually does.

If you are parenting a special child, journaling can help you deal with emotions that arise. Inner family work can be extremely valuable, and engaging your child in some form of expression through the arts (if appropriate and feasible) can work wonders. Some of the most powerful artwork I've ever seen was done at an art center for retarded children. The children at the center created exquisite greeting cards, painted, did sculpture and ceramics. Closer to home, my own kitchen is graced by some lovely ceramic vases created by a family friend, Sarah, who has Down's syndrome. Sarah's parents, Cathy and Baylis, are artists and introduced their children to the arts at an early age. Sarah's talent is unmistakable, and her parents were smart enough to encourage it. Sarah has a job and is her own person in every way. We all have a lot to learn from people like Sarah's and Jason's and Stevie Wonder's parents.

Over the years, many people who have parented special children have told me how invaluable the Creative Journal method was for them. One woman told me about the emotional roller-coaster ride she and her husband went on when they discovered that their child was physically handicapped and would never walk the way other children did. One by one, the mother examined her expectations, disbelief, disappointments, anger, resentment, self-pity, and on and on. She did all this by using her journal to explore her feelings. Through drawing and scribbling with crayons, she vented all her tumultuous emotions. Sometimes she cried the whole time she drew and wrote in her journal. "Many pages of my journal are tear-stained or wrinkled from pressing down so hard with the crayons," she told me. "Yet the inner peace I was able to arrive at, and the acceptance of my son for exactly who he is, made it all worthwhile." Her son later went on to become a child psychologist specializing in work with families dealing with life-threatening illnesses. The journal exercises for expressing feelings in Chapters 1 through 4 are excellent for working with the full range of emotions that are likely to come up if you are parenting a special child.

Another necessary ingredient for parents of challenged children has been a strong support system. Many of these parents I have met or worked with have told me that without their support team, they don't know how they would have survived. Whether it was a team of doctors; a counselor; a priest, minister, or rabbi; family members; friends; or organizations, these supporters provided encouragement, information, consolation, and love when it was most needed. Chapter 4 has many helpful exercises about the people in your life and building a support team.

TURNING TO THE CREATOR

In taking on the role of parent, you have assumed a great and holy task. Through Inner Family work in Chapter 3, you got in touch with the Nurturing and Protective Parents within. You found that these were necessary aspects of the self that, once actualized, could help you relate more lovingly with yourself and with your child. In Chapter 4, you wrote prayers to your Higher Power (God, the Creator, or whatever name you chose). It is my belief that experiencing the presence of this Higher Power will make all the difference in how you care for this precious life that has been given into your care. Children know this naturally. We need to constantly remind ourselves of this truth.

The directness and matter-of-fact nature of children's conversations about God always touch me. One summer, when my four grandsons were vacationing with me at my home, five-year-old Ian turned to me and suddenly asked, "Grandma, do you know God's telephone number?" After a pause in which I simply relished the question, I answered, "No, Ian. I don't need a telephone to talk to God. I talk to God in my heart." He smiled knowingly, perfectly satisfied with my response.

It has been my experience that faith in a power higher than ourselves gives us the strength we need in order to face all that parenting brings us (and all that life brings, too). Reliance on the spirit from which all life emanates is the best kind of support we could ever want. And wisdom from this spirit will be given if we will only ask.

In this last journal activity, you will be drawing and dialoguing with the Divine Creative Spirit in whatever form you see it and by whatever name you call it. I think of it as the ground of our being. You'll be drawing an image or a symbol and then asking for whatever guidance or help you need at this time. Listen carefully to that "still, small voice within." Take its words to heart.

All God's Children

Materials: Journal and felt pens

Purpose: To receive the guidance and grace of a power higher than yourself; to experience the presence of the Divine in your life

Activity:

1. With your *nondominant* hand, draw a picture or symbol for the Divine Creator, Higher Power (or whatever you call the source of all life).

2. With your *dominant* hand, ask your Higher Power for guidance, strength, or whatever quality you need at this time. If you need guidance about a particular issue or situation, ask for it. Be specific. Then allow your Higher Power to respond through writing done with your *nondominant* hand.

In times of doubt or pain, I urge you to turn to your Higher Power for guidance and solace. It will never fail you, but you must ask. Do it for your own sake. Do it for your child's sake as well.

10

Parenting in the Teen Years and Beyond

MOVING TOWARD ADULTHOOD

If you thought the changes of early childhood were dramatic, hold on to your seat. Adolescence is just as dramatic only more so, because the stakes are higher. Your child has gained a certain amount of independence while still remaining legally and financially dependent upon you. In fact, your child isn't considered a child anymore but is now known as an adolescent or a teenager. Of course, that doesn't mean he or she won't act like a child, even while developing an adult body. It simply means that everyone's expectations have changed.

The adolescent is *expected* to be more responsible, more thoughtful of others, more cooperative and mature than a child. And rightly so. By virtue of experience, age, and training, the teenager is expected to make better choices and decisions—for his own good and the good of others. I use the term *expected* gingerly because we all know that what we expect of teenagers and what they do are not necessarily the same thing. In some cases, they are diametrically opposed.

Let's face it, teenagers have a lot in common with two-year-olds, who are also learning to separate from their parents but at a different stage of development. The mantra of the two-year-old—"No, Mommy. Do it myself!"—reflects the same need that an adolescent has to separate from the family and find his own identity. He must experience life for himself in order to develop autonomy and an authentic sense of self.

At some deep level, the teenager must ask, "Who am I? How do I differ from my family? From my friends? How am I the same? Can I shape my own life? How do I go about doing that? Do I have to give up me in order to be loved by family and friends? And who is *me* anyway?" These are not easy questions to answer. As a therapist, I have observed that people who are living a self-reflective life never stop asking these questions. As a human being, I find that I ask some version of these questions every day of my life.

Now teenagers don't always ask these questions *consciously,* but they do and must ask them at some level. It is an inherent part of growing up and creating an adult life of one's own. Perhaps this questioning process only shows through behavior. The teenager rebels and acts contrary to her family's values and house rules. She wonders, "How will they react? Will I get into trouble? Will they stop loving me? Will they look the other way? What will happen if I'm different from my family?"

The same questions are being asked regarding the teenager's peer group. "How much like them must I be in order to be accepted? How different can I be and still be part of the group? Is there room to be an individual and still have friends?" We never really stop asking these questions, whether consciously or unconsciously. Yet it is in adolescence that these inquiries into identity versus society start to become articulated or acted out.

In addition to the age-old issues of adolescent developmental separation and rebellion, today's teens are facing dangers to their lives and health that haven't existed before. Parenting teenagers in a world of fast cars, drug and alcohol abuse, easy sex, AIDS and HIV-positive, and chat room pickup action on the Internet is a huge challenge. Easy access to guns, explosives, and other weapons has created an atmosphere of fear and anxiety for parents and children alike. The environment is not teen-friendly, and parents of adolescents have precious little support.

Regarding the issue of sexuality, for example, the mainstream culture and media are obsessed with images of superficial sex, and then we blame teenagers for unwanted pregnancies. The image being broadcast to young people is that a teenage girl must look sexy in order to be loved and accepted. Today's fashion magazines (which strongly shape the self-image and body image of adolescent girls) would at one time have been described as soft porn. Half the time, you can't even tell what the ad is selling. The clothes hardly show. But the bodies are all over the place. And the models are mostly teenagers themselves.

A recent television documentary on the modeling industry pointed out that by their mid-twenties, many models are has-beens. The half-starved waif look we see in female models depends upon and promotes a culture of anorexia, bulimia, and other eating disorders, yet we uphold this "look" as the ideal for feminine beauty. It is a known fact that movie stars, entertainers, and models suffer a disproportionate percentage of eating disorders compared to the rest of the population. We send mixed messages to adolescent girls, and then we wonder why some of them are "mixed up" about sexuality, their bodies, relationships, and more.

On the positive side, the women's movement of the seventies gave young women more equal opportunities regarding career choices and lifestyle options. Parents of today's teenagers were raised with a far more open attitude about what is possible. They can be strong role models for finding the work one truly loves and is best suited for.

As for adolescent boys, they face the same challenges and dangers that girls face—drugs and alcohol abuse, unsafe sex, reckless driving, and the use of weapons. Boys may also face heavy pressure in our workaholic society to overachieve in sports, in school, and in the world. Some rebel, while others succumb to the pressure. The ones who adopt workaholism and material affluence as the path to acceptance often fall into the trap of other addictions as well. Or their health and relationships suffer. On the other hand, the rebels end up as "slackers," or they act out in violence. Some youngsters do both. They may get on a high-achievement track only to sabotage themselves through accidents, addictions, or other destructive behavior.

Fortunately, there are also many wonderful resources for teens who are in trouble: twelve-step programs for addiction, community and school counseling services, church programs, and more. We just need to heed the warning signs and help youngsters avail themselves of these services before it's too late. I've worked with many clients and students in their twenties and thirties who were already veterans of recovery programs for drugs and alcohol and were creating a productive, fulfilling life for themselves. For people so young, their level of self-reflection and insight has always amazed me.

I have asked many parents of teenagers today how they do it. I often get answers like "I pray a lot" or "It sure brings you closer to God" or "My teenager is what got me into therapy when nothing else could, so I guess I'm grateful." Parents often tell me that they began keeping a journal when their children entered adolescence. They say things like "Journaling saved my life when my kids hit their teens" or "If it hadn't been for my journal, I would have gone stark, raving mad."

Now I don't want to paint only a bleak picture about parenting teenagers. There are moments that are sheer bliss. The graduation ceremony, the signs of talent and abilities that will shape a young person's future work in the world, the thank-you note, the companionship and shared experiences that one can have only with a teenager—these are memories that last forever.

LETTING GO

For a parent, the learning curve has to do with letting go while still being there for your teenager. Your child is a separate being, with a destiny of his own, with unique opportunities and risks, and with his own life to live. Trying to control the outcomes of your child's choices is neither possible nor healthy (for you or the teenager). Your teenager is going to be making lots of choices (including many you don't approve of) and lots of mistakes. There will be values collisions as well, as your teenager starts to think and decide for himself.

There will also be ample opportunity to live the example you want to teach. No one is more aware of hypocrisy than adolescents. They can spot duplicity a mile away. So telling teenagers to behave one way while we act in another (perhaps opposite) way just won't work. When I taught parents of teenagers on probation, the biggest dilemma my coteacher and I faced was the hypocrisy of the parents. My coteacher worked with the kids, while I led groups for the parents. Their children had been arrested for drugs, but as it turned out, most of the parents were themselves heavy drinkers or abusers of pharmaceutical drugs. The kids would say things like: "My dad's bombed every night on martinis. My mom's always popping pills of some kind. But they're always preaching to me about drugs. What's the difference? Is it just about what's legal or not? Isn't getting high the same thing, no matter what you use?" Good questions. These kids were only following in their parents' footsteps.

Teenagers will keep you honest if you let them. It can be exasperating, but it can also be a great opportunity for growth. Your child's teenage years can be a wonderful time for you to find your true self, too. As your adolescent is preparing for adulthood and a life separate from yours, you can prepare for the eventual time when you face the "empty-nest syndrome." If you have allowed yourself to separate from your teenager while your teenager gradually separates from you, the empty-nest syndrome won't hit you nearly as hard. You will already have begun the process.

Looking back to your own experiences of adolescence can help you develop compassion and understanding for your adolescent child. Those turning points and decisions you faced during your teenage years can give you valuable insights into the challenges your teenager is dealing with. Revisiting your adolescence can also help you better understand yourself today. If you discover some choices you made in adolescence that don't serve you now, you can explore other possibilities.

A good example of how this works is Tom, a successful insurance broker who was pressuring his sixteen-year-old son, Brad, to go to law school. Brad was a good student and hard worker, but there was one big problem. He didn't want to be a lawyer.

His heart was set on becoming a research scientist. Tom told himself that he only "wanted the best for his son" (meaning the affluence and status he associated with the practice of law). When it came time for Brad to apply to college, they began having terrible arguments about the boy's future.

Through journaling, Tom discovered that he had wanted to be a lawyer when he was Brad's age. His family had discouraged him because of the expense of law school, so he went into business instead. Now, at some unconscious level, he wanted Brad to live out his dream. When he discovered what he'd been doing, Tom stopped pressuring Brad and in fact apologized for his behavior. They became far closer than they had ever been, and Tom could then support his son's authentic choice of a career based on his genuine interests and talents.

When I Was Your Age

Materials: Journal and felt pens; family photos from your teenage years

Purpose: To become aware of your feelings about being an adolescent; to revisit critical moments from your teenage years

Activity:
1. If you have any family photos of yourself as a teenager, sit and look through them. If one of them especially attracts your attention, study it carefully. How old were you? Are you alone or with others? What's going on in the picture? What was going on at that time in your life? How do you feel looking at this photo? Write your observations in your journal, using your *dominant* hand.
2. With your *nondominant* hand, draw a picture of yourself as a teenager. Portray yourself at the same age your teenage child is now. Picture yourself in an actual situation that stands out in your memory.

3. With your *nondominant* hand, write down your feelings about that time in your life (the situation you portrayed in your drawing). What was happening at that time in your life? How did you feel about it at the time? What decisions did you make? What actions did you take? Write about it.

4. With your *nondominant* hand, let the teenager that you were (in either the photo or the drawing) write a letter in your journal to your adolescent son or daughter today. Remember, this is only for your eyes, so you can say whatever you wish.

5. If you are having a conflict with your teenager, with your *dominant* hand, write about any similar situations you faced during your own adolescence. What was the situation you faced? How did you feel about it? What did you do? How do you feel about it now? What did you learn from the experience? Would you have done anything differently? Describe it.

LINES OF COMMUNICATION

Even though children develop verbal skills when they go to school, communication with parents and other adults often breaks down when they reach adolescence. In the separation process, the teenager may want more privacy and some "mental room of her own," to paraphrase the title of a book by Virginia Woolf. This can include a growing territoriality about one's own room and possessions in an attempt to carve out one's individual psychic space and identity. It can also mean communicating less with parents and more with peers.

Sometimes our feelings get hurt because our teenagers prefer spending more and more time with their friends or are engaged in activities away from home, such as sports and clubs. If we don't explore our own feelings about this, we may disguise them with judgment of our kids, their interests, and their companions. That doesn't mean that we don't have boundaries and limits regarding whom our children hang around with and where they spend their time. If you know one of your daughter's friends is using drugs, you certainly would discourage such a friendship.

Letting go does not mean abdicating responsibility or not protecting your teenager from harm. You and your child also have legal consequences to deal with, so you must protect your child as much as possible. As a minor, she is your responsibility. It's a delicate balance, and there are no easy answers. You have to be the judge about where protecting stops and controlling begins. You need to distinguish between serving your teenager's best interests and indulging your old emotional garbage that needs to be cleared.

Let me give an example of old "stuff" from a parent's childhood that got in the way of current communication. Elise and her husband were parenting their teenage son, Joel. Elise had never faced her deep-seated fear of abandonment. When she was fifteen, Elise's father had divorced her mother and moved to another city. Elise's deep wound of abandonment was now being activated in her relationship with her son.

During his childhood, Joel had been very close to Elise, sharing common interests in computer technology and science. At fifteen (the same age Elise was when her parents divorced), Joel started spending more time with his pals than he did at home. This triggered Elise's old feelings of loss, which she covered up by becoming critical of Joel's friends and activities that took him away from her. Through journaling and some counseling, Elise was able to separate her needs from her son's normal desire to develop friendships outside the family. She did some re-parenting on herself and developed a wonderful support system and new friendships that helped her through the empty-nest syndrome. Her relationship with Joel improved, and family life became harmonious again.

A parent who doesn't know where his or her feelings are coming from may cover up vulnerability (fear, sadness, or grief over loss) with platitudes, preaching, or punishment. But teenagers aren't stupid. They can usually see through these masquerades, even if they don't know where the cover-up is coming from. In therapy, I've heard adolescents poke all kinds of holes in a parent's argument that "You should stay home more." The more preachy and heavy-handed the parent was, the more rebellious the teenager became, of course. When the past is healed, the present relationship with the teenage daughter or son can become healthier. Facing our fears and our grief from the past takes courage, but the payoff is immense. There are many journal activities from Chapters 2 through 4 that can be useful for dealing with your own issues from the past. Find the ones that fit for you at any given time.

Teen Talk

Materials: Journal and felt pens

Purpose: To become aware of your feelings about parenting your adolescent child; to explore your relationship with your teenager

Activity:

1. With your *nondominant* hand, write down your feelings about your role as parent to your teenager. What do you fear the most? Does any of your teenager's behavior make you angry or resentful? Are you satisfied with the relationship with your teenager? What do you like most about it? What do you like least?

2. With your *nondominant* hand, draw a picture that portrays your relationship with your teenage child. Then write your observations with your *dominant* hand.

3. If you aren't happy with the relationship, draw a new picture with your *nondominant* hand. Show how you'd like the relationship to be. With your *dominant* hand, write about the kind of relationship you would like with your adolescent son or daughter.

4. With your *dominant* hand, make a list of the things your teenager does that bother or upset you. Then take each one and construct a sentence that expresses how that behavior affects you. These are called "I messages" because they focus on you and your feelings rather than blaming

and name-calling directed at the teenager. For example: "When you come home late at night two hours after our agreed-upon curfew, I start feeling terrified that you may have been in an accident."

Note: For more information about sending I messages, see Dr. Tom Gordon's book *Parent Effectiveness Training.*

5. With your *dominant* hand, make a list in your journal of all the things you appreciate about your teenager. Then write a real letter to your teenager expressing the things you appreciate and enjoy about him or her and actually mail it.

Sometimes Anthony and I are on different planets. He seems to be all over the place—physically (he's so tall now!) and emotionally. Like when he leaves stuff all over the house (something he never did much of when he was younger). At those times I try to stay calm and hold my boundaries firm. But I'm filled with questions. Is he regressing? In some ways he's acting more like a pre-schooler than an adolescent.

At other times, we take time and talk (if I can get him to fit me in between ball games, homework, his friends and part time job). When we do talk, there's a really nice flow betweeen us. We talk about what's going on in the world: politics, wars, violence in schools, what's happening at work, etc. And when the chips are down, like when his teacher died last semester and Anthony's grades were suffering afterward, we can always get to the heart of the matter. We really love each other and we both know it. The other day, after a talk about girls, he said, "You know, Mom, my other friends are amazed that I can talk to you about this stuff. They can't talk to their mothers about the stuff that I do. Thanks." Wow, did THAT feel good!

LISTENING TO YOURSELF, LISTENING TO YOUR TEENAGER

One thing teenagers often tell counselors is that nobody listens to them. Everyone talks at them, preaches, and tells them how to live their lives. Yet they don't feel heard. And nobody is helping them find their own way. One of the most important skills I learned when I was trained as a Parent Effectiveness Instructor for Dr. Thomas Gordon was called active listening. It can work miracles in a relationship. The practice of active listening develops an open mind and an open heart. It is based on the belief that other people can know what is best for them if they are encouraged to look within themselves.

Here's how it works. In active listening, we provide feedback through paraphrasing to the other person what we hear her saying. She feels heard, but most important, we hear what she *really* feels and thinks, not what we *assume* she feels and thinks. It takes a lot of the guesswork out of relating. Active listening honors our differences and the uniqueness of our individual experiences while fostering understanding and compassion. Active listening can bring you much closer to your child.

Jolene used active listening with Janie, her fifteen-year-old daughter. Janie came storming into the kitchen after school one day and threw her books onto the table without saying a word to her mother. Instead of lecturing Janie about manners, Jolene took this as a cue to listen.

> JOLENE: You really look upset. Want to talk about it?
>
> JANIE: Upset? Yeah, I am. I'm furious.
>
> JOLENE: Looks like something happened at school that made you mad.
>
> JANIE: Well, not at school exactly. It's my friend Katie. She was supposed to drive me to the game. I waited forty-five minutes for her, and she never showed up. So I missed it.
>
> JOLENE: You must be disappointed. You were really looking forward to this game.
>
> JANIE: Yeah! What a bummer. [*Sits down at the table looking dejected. After a while, she looks up at her mom.*] I guess I better call Katie and find out what happened. [*Goes to the phone and has a brief conversation with Katie, whose engine had died on the way to picking Janie up. After hearing that it couldn't be helped, Janie comes back and talks more about her disappointment over missing the game. Then she goes on about her day. The feelings have been cleared.*]

Another scenario might have involved Jolene's chiding Janie for not greeting her when she came home. Or she might have tried to "fix" Janie by offering her something to eat or do to avoid her feelings. Or she might have told Janie to cheer up (negating her real feelings). Instead, Jolene lent an open ear and allowed her daughter to own her true feelings of disappointment. This enabled Janie to get into and through the feelings much faster than if Jolene had tried to make them go away.

One friend of mine who used this approach in raising an adolescent boy on her own is Marilyn Hamlin, an actress and a social worker. Marilyn shared with me a beautiful letter she wrote to a friend who was struggling to raise a teenager. Here's an excerpt from that letter:

I am a firm believer in doing what your child might ask . . . if I can do it. You know—well-meaning "helpful" people are often NOT HELPFUL AT ALL because they are doing what makes them feel good and could care less about whether it is REALLY HELPFUL to the person they want to appear to help.

This has been the big challenge of my motherhood . . . to ask James what would be helpful, then give it to him, if I can, and to constantly check with him to see if it is REALLY HELPFUL. Yes, it is hurtful when he says, "STOP, this isn't helpful after all," but it is the truest principle of helping our children. If James says it's no longer helpful—I must STOP and ask, "What would be helpful now?" and I must give up my own way of helping and be guided by him. I MUST if I am to be truly helpful to my son.

I guess what hurts about giving up my own notion of what is helpful is—MY EGO HURTS. My own false sense that I know what is better for another person than they can know for themselves. Remember, it's "written in his heart" and he can access that if he's supported in a way that gives him enough credit to make some safe mistakes. AND then supported to learn from those mistakes . . . not punished for the mistake and not punished with no credit.

For me this is the other area of my relationship with my son that is difficult to tolerate: I must hold my position, my opinion, while I see him head for a mistake. I choose to let him make the mistake. I choose to stand by while he suffers (pain, embarrassment, anger) from his mistake and to not step in until he asks for my help.

This is principle's way of teaching. It carries its own reward for right action and its own consequences for wrong action. And it is our child's better teacher than us humanly foibled parents: Principle never fails.

When or if he asks for my help, I do not rush to give it, but find out first what kind of help he would like me to give. I do not seek to add insult to injury by pointing out he made a mistake. He is acutely aware of that! And I cannot always do what he asks me to do to help—so we discuss it. TALK IS IMPORTANT.

This is where I have found the most growth and development in our relationship . . . when I take the time to tell him why I can't do what he asks . . . or when I get clarification on just how he wants my help. (This is a tricky one because parents are often a few steps ahead as the child struggles to explain his or her mistake and . . . need for help.) . . . I think life is best lived within a healthfully supportive environment of trial and error, problem-solving and discovery!

A wonderful way to learn from our own trials and errors is to engage in problem solving and discovery in the journal. A great technique for doing this is to write conversations with the significant people in our lives. We can gain greater understanding of ourselves but also tap into a deep intuitive knowingness about the other person. The next activity will give you more practice in listening, first to yourself and then to another.

Pen Pals

Materials: Journal and felt pens

Purpose: To become aware of the dynamics of your relationship with your teenager; to open up understanding and compassion

Activity:

1. Using both hands, write a conversation with your teenager. With your *dominant* hand, ask your teenager how she feels about you and about your relationship. Let the voice of your teenager write through your *nondominant* hand. Then continue the conversation and tell your teenager how you feel about the relationship. Again, write your voice with your *dominant* hand. Go back and forth with the conversation, alternating hands, until you feel the conversation is complete.

2. Write a letter to your teenager in your journal using your *dominant* hand. Tell your teenager what she means to

you. Tell her how you feel about the conversation you had in step 1 and what kind of insights you gained from having this journal talk.

———————

As you observe your adolescent, it is important to notice your reactions to his behavior, to his changing needs, and your ability to support his growth. As in the earlier years of parenting, you will probably question your abilities as a parent. Adolescents can feel like such a giant responsibility, especially when they make *big* mistakes. Uncertainty, fatigue, anger, fear, doubt, and confusion may all be jumbled up together. The range of emotions that come up is immense. Journaling can take you a long way toward feeling the feelings, accepting them, and expressing them safely and creatively. Journaling can also help you better relate with your adolescent child, as it promotes clearer thinking and more honest heart-to-heart communication, first with yourself and then with your youngster.

TRUST AND SAFETY, AUTONOMY AND COOPERATION

In developing better communication with yourself and then with your teenager, you are strengthening safety and trust. This is good preparation for the next stage—adulthood—in which your son or daughter will hopefully move toward independence. Honoring your son for who he is, cherishing your daughter as a unique individual will make it safe to be with you. Comparing your teenager to others erodes the trust between you, as your child will feel negated. Our children cannot be poured into a mold of our making, and they will resist with all their might, thank God! So if your child fights back when your ego takes control, be grateful. God is working through the situation and confronting you with "tough love."

I'll repeat something I said in Chapter 9: No child likes feeling that she is not OK the way she is but would be lovable "if only" she measured up to some *ideal* or expectation of yours. (In fact, no adult likes to feel that way either. We all want acceptance, regardless of how old we are.) A judgmental environment simply isn't a safe place to be oneself. If you focus on knowing and fulfilling yourself, you won't be tempted to live out your unrealized dreams through your kids. If you want to dance or start a business or travel to China, then *do it*. Don't push your teenager to be a dancer, businessman, or world traveler.

The Creative Journal is a perfect tool for helping you find and live from what is most important to you personally. Realize yourself and your own talents and you give a wonderful example to your teenager. Living well is the best role modeling you can offer. Whether your teenager takes the hint or not is beyond your control, but at least you've done your part. In staying focused on your own life and needs, I recommend revisiting earlier exercises that are appropriate for you, especially the ones having to do with self-nurturing, Inner Family work, and creating harmony within yourself and your home (Chapters 2 through 4).

As you practice communicating with yourself and with your teenager, hopefully the level of cooperation will grow as well. Your adolescent will be more likely to take on more responsibility, share in more household chores, and prepare himself for being on his own. This all takes place gradually over the years, and when your teenager has grown into an adult, the years of preparation will start to pay off. Paradoxical as it may seem, a cooperative person can also be a more autonomous one. There will always be rules and regulations to follow in the large adult world, the needs of other people to consider (whether they be the landlord, boss, neighbor, or mortgage company). The sooner teenagers learn this, the better off they are. Although they may rebel against your rules, we live in a world of laws and regulations, and young people need to learn this early on.

Boundaries and Limits

Materials: Journal and felt pens

Purpose: To become aware of your limits and boundaries in relation to your teenager; to clarify your values and ground rules in relation to your child's current needs and behavior

Activity:

1. With your *dominant* hand, write about your teenager's current level of responsibility regarding the household, family members, school, work, and so forth. Write a list of the things he or she is responsible for. Do you experience any conflict around your teenager's level of responsibilities? Write about it with your *dominant* hand. What can you do to help your teenager be more responsible? Write about it using your *nondominant* hand. If you're not sure, ask your child.

2. With your *dominant* hand, write a letter in your journal. Address it to your teenager and tell him or her what you discovered in step 1 of this activity.

3. With your *dominant* hand, write a letter stating clearly what your boundaries and limits are regarding your teenager's behavior. Describe what you accept and what you don't accept about his or her values and behavior. If there are values differences between you, write about them.

THE FINE ART OF LIMITS AND BOUNDARIES

Journaling is an excellent way to reexamine your values and get clear on everyone's current needs. Chapters 1 and 2 as well as 4 can help you reconsider your expectations and rules. As mentioned in Chapter 9, you are living in a family setting. Everything cannot revolve around your teenager. Rules, limits, and boundaries must still prevail, no matter what your teenager thinks or says—and no matter what his or her peers are doing or other parents are saying. Be true to yourself and your needs.

Some *behaviors* will simply be unacceptable to you, especially if they are illegal or injurious to your child's health. Expectations need to be communicated clearly and reinforced with consistency. Using your journal to evaluate your ground rules, limits, and boundaries regarding off-limits places, people, and situations is a valuable means for clarifying your expectations. Teenagers may resist, complain, and rebel, but they still need clear boundaries to provide security and a sense of limits. Freedom is not license to go out of control. It is earned through responsibility. You may want to return to Chapter 9 and do some of those journal activities again. The same principles apply, but at a different level of growth.

Creative Time Together

Materials: Journal and felt pens; photo collage materials and art paper ($18\frac{1}{2}" \times 24"$)

Purpose: To spend time together in creative activities; to express shared values through creative visioning

Activity:
1. Make a series of photo collages in your journal of what is important in your life at this time. Then portray the experiences you want to create in your life. Write down your observations on a separate page using your *dominant* hand.
2. Invite your teenager (and the rest of the family) to create photo collages together, beginning with each person's making an individual collage about what is important to him or her.
3. Invite your family to do a collaborative collage on the same piece of paper. Your theme might be a vacation or trip you plan to take together, a family project (renovating the garage or planting a garden). Have each person contribute what he or she would like to see in the finished project or the shared experience.
4. Talk to your teenager about the experiences you've had with journaling. If she is not already keeping a journal, find out whether she would be interested in doing so. If the answer is yes, offer whatever support your teenager would like—a blank book, set of pens, and so on. You might consider giving him or her a copy of my book *The Creative Journal for Teens.*
5. Draw a series of cartoon pictures with your *nondominant* hand showing your child growing up from infancy to the

present time. What were the key experiences you have had or observations you have made of your child's uniqueness and special moments in his or her life?

6. Make a new collage called "Our Family" using magazine photos, snapshots, or other images. If you like, include pictures or symbols of your extended family and support system, other family members, and so forth. You may want to do these collages in a memory scrapbook or photo album as well.

Dance, music, art projects, and plays are also excellent forms of shared experiences with teenagers. Don't forget to play together. Laughter and fun are like glue that brings people together.

PARENTING YOUR GROWN CHILD

Everything that has been said about parenting young children and teenagers applies at a new level when your son or daughter is all grown up. Many of the journal activities presented throughout this book will be applicable when you are dealing with new issues, such as your son's or daughter's career choices, relationships, and other major life decisions. You will always be your child's parent (even when you become a grandparent), but the relationship moves to a new level. More separation, more autonomy, but (if you've done your homework) more under-standing and compassion. Mutual support becomes more likely as time goes on. And as your children have more life experience under their belt, they will probably look at you with new eyes. As my younger daughter, Aleta, said to me after she started rais-ing her own children, "How did you do it, Mom?" She'd gained a new respect for parenting because she was knee-deep in it. She could forgive my mistakes because she was making her own. And she was learning, as I had, from her own children.

My last bit of advice is this: *Don't forget to pray.*

Parenting is too difficult a task to do on your own. You are not alone. The Creator of all is there for you, ready to support you in this sacred task of bringing a life into the world and nurturing his or her unique expression. Write your prayers, sing them, dance them, say them quietly to yourself. Tap into that reservoir of love and life that allowed you to become a parent in the first place.

In that spirit, I leave you with this prayer of blessing:

May your life be blessed.
May the Divine Creator be honored through you and your
    family.
May you be ever thankful
    for the gift of life
    for the gift of your child
    and for the creativity that has been showered upon you.
        Amen

ACKNOWLEDGMENTS

Many people contributed to the creation of this book. Special thanks to my dear friend and associate Mara Sanders for field-testing the manuscript in journal groups for parents. She has supported my work with great love and creativity, applying these principles in her counseling practice.

I am deeply grateful to those who joined Mara's groups and provided me with the wonderful journal and art examples that illustrate this book. The drawings, collages, and journal writings appearing in these pages were contributed by:

Rosemary Adams
Caroline Barry
Norma Cardenas
Aleta Pearce Francis
Marsha Gamel
Marilyn Hamlin
Christine Keebler
Jade Larios
Jim Ogden
Maricruz Rodriquez
Sonia Rodriguez

Lori Spencer
Adela Steinman
Sherri Watton
Susan Winer

Thanks to Marsha Gamel and Penny Sannella for sharing their adoption experiences with me. Thanks as well to Shambhala Publications, for their support of my work and for publishing a quality of books and authors with whom it is an honor to be associated; and to my editors, Emily Hilburn Sell and Joel Segel, and designers, Graciela Galup and Ruth Kolbert.

BIBLIOGRAPHY

SELF-CARE AND JOURNALING

BENSON, HERBERT. *Relaxation Response.* Avenal, N.J.: Outlet Book Co., 1993.

CAPACCHIONE, LUCIA. *The Creative Journal: The Art of Finding Yourself.* Athens: Ohio University/Swallow Press, 1979.

———. *The Picture of Health: Healing Your Life with Art.* Van Nuys, Calif.: Newcastle Publishing, 1996.

———. *The Picture of Health: Meditation and Guided Writing/Drawing Exercises* (audiotape). Carson, Calif.: Hay House, 1992.

———. *Recovery of Your Inner Child.* New York: Simon and Schuster/Fireside, 1991.

———. *Visioning: Ten Steps to Designing the Life of Your Dreams.* New York: Tarcher/Putnam, 2000.

———. *Well-Being Journal.* Van Nuys, Calif.: Newcastle Publishing, 1989.

CARLSON, RICHARD. *Don't Sweat the Small Stuff . . . And It's All Small Stuff.* New York: Hyperion, 1997.

KEEL, PHILIPP. *All About Me.* New York: Broadway Books, 1998.

NORTHRUP, CHRISTIANE. *Women's Bodies, Women's Wisdom.* New York: Bantam, 1994.

THE CHILD BEFORE AND DURING BIRTH!

CHAMBERLAIN, DAVID. *Babies Remember Birth—And Other Scientific Discoveries about the Mind and Personality of Your Newborn.* New York: Ballantine Books, 1990.

LEBOYER, FREDERICK. *Birth without Violence.* New York: Fawcett Columbine, 1990.

NILSSON, LENNART. *A Child Is Born.* New York: Delacorte Press/Seymour Lawrence, 1990. (Photographs of fetal development.)

VERNY, THOMAS, WITH JOHN KELLY. *The Secret Life of the Unborn Child.* New York: Delacorte Press, 1990.

VERNY, THOMAS, AND PAMELA WEINTRAUB. *Nurturing the Unborn Child: A Nine-Month Program of Soothing, Stimulating and Communicating with Your Baby.* New York: Bantam Doubleday Dell, 1991.

PREGNANCY AND CHILDBIRTH

ARMSTRONG, PENNY, AND SHERYL FELDMAN. *A Wise Birth: Bringing Together the Best of Natural Childbirth and Modern Medicine.* New York: William Morrow, 1990.

BALDWIN, RAHIMA. *Special Delivery: The Complete Guide to Informed Birth.* Berkeley, Calif.: Celestial Arts, 1986.

BALDWIN, RAHIMA, AND TERRA PALMIERI. *Pregnant Feelings: Developing Trust in Birth.* 2d ed. Berkeley, Calif.: Celestial Arts, 1990.

DICK-READ, GRANTLY. *Childbirth without Fear: The Original Approach to Natural Childbirth.* Rev. ed. Edited by Helen Weisel and Harlan F. Ellis. New York: HarperCollins, 1987.

DUNHAM, CARROLL, AND THE BODY SHOP TEAM. *Mamatoto: A Celebration of Birth.* New York: Penguin Books, 1992.

EDWARDS, MARGOT, AND MARY WALDORF. *Reclaiming Birth: History and Heroines of American Childbirth Reform.* Trumansburg, N.Y.: The Crossing Press, 1984.

EISENBERG, ARLENE, SANDEE HATHAWAY, AND HEIDI E. MURKOFF. *What to Expect When You're Expecting.* New York: Workman, 1991.

HARPER, BARBARA. *Gentle Birth Choices.* Rochester, Vt.: Inner Traditions, 1994.

JONES, CARL. *Mind over Labor.* New York: Penguin Books, 1987.

———. *Visualizations for an Easier Childbirth.* Deephaven, Minn.: Meadowbrook, 1988.

KITZINGER, SHEILA. *Birth over Thirty.* Rev. ed. New York: Penguin Books, 1985.

———. *The Complete Book of Pregnancy and Childbirth.* New York: Knopf, 1980.

———. *Your Baby, Your Way: Making Pregnancy Decisions and Birth Plans.* New York: Pantheon Books, 1987.

KNIGHT, MARY. *Love Letters before Birth and Beyond: A Mother's*

Journal to Read and to Keep. Traverse City, Mich.: Single Eye Publishing, 1997.

MITFORD, JESSICA. *The American Way of Birth.* New York: Penguin, 1992.

SIMKIN, PENNY, JANET WHALLEY, AND ANNE KEPPLER. *Pregnancy, Childbirth and the Newborn: A Complete Guide for Expectant Parents.* Deephaven, Minn.: Meadowbrook Press, 1984.

STILLERMAN, ELAINE. *Mother Massage: A Handbook for Relieving the Discomforts of Pregnancy.* New York: Bantam Doubleday Dell, 1992.

PHYSICAL EXERCISE AND NUTRITION FOR PREGNANCY

BING, ELISABETH. *Elisabeth Bing's Guide to Moving through Pregnancy.* New York: Farrar, Straus, and Giroux, 1992.

BREWER, GAIL SFORZA, AND TOM BREWER. *What Every Pregnant Woman Should Know: The Truth about Drugs and Diet in Pregnancy.* New York: Viking Penguin, 1986.

NOBLE, ELIZABETH. *Essential Exercises for the Childbearing Years.* Rev. ed. Boston: Houghton Mifflin, 1982.

OLKIN, SYLVIA KLEIN. *Positive Parenting Fitness.* New York: Avery, 1992.

———. *Positive Pregnancy Fitness.* New York: Avery, 1987.

PARVATI-BAKER, JEANNINE. *Prenatal Yoga and Natural Birth.* Berkeley, Calif.: North Atlantic Books, 1986.

MIDWIVES AND DOULAS

GASKIN, INA MAE. *Spiritual Midwifery.* Summertown, Tenn.: The Book Publishing Co., 1980.

HALLET, ELIZABETH, AND KAREN EHRLICH. *Midwife Means with Woman: A Guide to Healthy Childbearing.* California Association of Midwives, 1991.

JONES, CARL. *Alternative Birth: The Complete Guide.* Los Angeles: Tarcher, 1991.

KLAUS, MARSHALL H. *Mothering the Mother: How a Doula Can Help You Have a Shorter, Easier, Healthier Birth.* Reading, Mass.: Addison-Wesley, 1993.

PANUTHOS, CLAUDIA. *Transformation through Birth: A Woman's Guide.* New York: Bergin and Garvey, 1984.

PEREZ, PAULINA, AND CHERYL SNEDEKER. *Special Women: The Role of the Professional Labor Assistant*. Seattle, Wash.: Pennypress, 1990.

PETERSON, GAYLE. *An Easier Childbirth: A Mother's Guide for Birthing Normally*. 2d ed. Berkeley, Calif.: Shadow and Light Publications, 1993.

BREAST-FEEDING, TOUCH, AND INFANT MASSAGE

HEINL, TINA. *Baby Massage: Shared Growth through the Hands*. Boston: Sigo Press, 1991.

HUGGINS, KATHLEEN. *The Nursing Mother's Companion*. Rev. ed. Boston: Harvard Common Press, 1991.

LA LECHE LEAGUE. *The Womanly Art of Breastfeeding*. Franklin Park, N.Y.: Interstate Printers and Publishers, 1991.

MCCLURE, VIMALA SCHNIEDER. *Infant Massage: A Handbook for Loving Parents*. New York: Bantam, 1989.

RENFREW, MARY, CHLOE FISHER, AND SUZANNE ARMS. *Breastfeeding*. Berkeley, Calif.: Celestial Arts, 1990.

RELATIONSHIPS FOR COUPLES AND PARTNERS IN PARENTING

CAPACCHIONE, LUCIA. *The Power of Your Other Hand*. Van Nuys, Calif.: Newcastle, 1988. (Chapter on "Reaching Out: Dialogues with Others.")

———. *The Wisdom of Your Other Hand* (set of five audiotapes). Boulder, Colo.: Sounds True, 1994. (Tapes on *The Inner Family* and *The Relationship Dance*.)

CARLSON, RICHARD. *Don't Sweat the Small Stuff with Your Family: Simple Ways to Keep Daily Responsibilities and Household Chores from Taking Over Your Life*. New York: Hyperion, 1998.

HENDRICKS, HARVILLE. *Getting the Love You Want: A Guide for Couples*. New York: Harper Perennial, 1988.

JONES, CARL. *Sharing Birth: A Father's Guide to Giving Support during Labor*. Granby, Mass.: Bergin and Garvey, 1989.

JONES, CARL, AND JAN JONES. *The Birth Partner's Handbook*. Deephaven, Minn.: Meadowbrook, 1989.

SCHWARTZ, LENI. *Bonding before Birth: A Guide to Becoming a Family*. Boston: Sigo Press, 1991.

SIMKIN, PENNY. *The Birth Partner: Everything You Need to Know to Help a Woman through Childbirth*. Boston: Harvard Common Press, 1989.

STONE, HAL, AND SIDRA WINKELMAN. *Embracing Each Other: Rela-*

tionship as Teacher, Healer and Guide. San Rafael, Calif.: New
World Library, 1989.

TESSINA, TINA, AND RILEY K. SMITH. *True Partners: A Workbook for
Building a Lasting Intimate Relationship.* New York: Tarcher/Per-
igee, 1993.

VISSELL, BARRY, AND JOYCE VISSELL. *The Shared Heart: Relationship,
Initiations and Celebration.* Oakland, Calif.: Ramira Publishing,
1984.

WELWOOD, JOHN. *Journey of the Heart: Intimate Relationship and
the Path of Love.* New York: HarperCollins, 1990.

PARENTING AND CHILD DEVELOPMENT

BRAZELTON, T. BERRY. *Families: Crisis and Caring.* Reading, Mass.:
Addison-Wesley, 1989.

CLARKE, JEAN ILLSLEY. *Self-Esteem: A Family Affair.* Center City,
Minn.: Hazelden, 1998.

CLARKE, JEAN ILLSLEY, AND CONNIE DAWSON. *Growing Up Again:
Parenting Ourselves, Parenting Our Children.* Center City, Minn.:
Hazelden, 1998.

DREIKURS, RUDOLPH, AND VICKI STOLTZ. *Children: The Challenge.*
New York: NAL-Dutton, 1987.

GIBRAN, KAHLIL. *The Prophet.* New York: Knopf, 1956. (Sections on
love, marriage, and children.)

GORDON, THOMAS. *P.E.T.: Parent Effectiveness Training.* New York:
New American Library, 1975.

JONES, SANDY. *Crying Baby, Sleepless Nights: Why Your Baby Is Crying and What You Can Do about It.* Boston: Harvard Common
Press, 1992.

LEACH, PENELOPE. *The First Six Months: Getting Together with Your
Baby.* New York: Knopf, 1987.

NELSON, JANE, CHERYL ERWIN, AND ROSLYN DUFFY. *Positive Discipline for Preschoolers.* Rocklin, Calif.: Prima Publishing, 1995.

RYCE, KAREN. *Parenting for the New Millennium.* Rohnert Park,
Calif.: HU Enterprises, 1996.

SAMUELS, MICHAEL, AND NANCY SAMUELS. *The Well Baby Book.*
New York: Summit Books, 1979.

SEARS, WILLIAM. *The Fussy Baby: How to Bring Out the Best in Your
High Need Child.* New York: NAL-Dutton, 1985.

———. *Keys to Caring and Preparing for Your New Baby.* Haupauge,
N.Y.: Barron's Educational Series, 1991.

SEARS, WILLIAM, AND MARTHA SEARS. *The Baby Book: Everything
You Need to Know about Your Baby—From Birth to Age Two.*
Boston: Little, Brown, 1993.

WELTER, PAUL. *Learning from Children*. Wheaton, Ill.: Tyndale House, 1984.

YOUR CHILD'S CREATIVITY, EDUCATION, AND SPIRITUALITY

BROOKES, MONA. *Drawing for Older Children and Teens*. Los Angeles: Tarcher, 1991.
———. *Drawing with Children*. Rev. and expanded. New York: Tarcher/Putnam, 1996.
CAPACCHIONE, LUCIA. *The Creative Journal for Children: A Guide for Parents, Teachers, and Counselors*. Boston: Shambhala Publications, 1989. (For ages five to fifteen.)
———. *The Creative Journal for Teens*. Van Nuys, Calif.: Newcastle, 1992.
COLES, ROBERT. *The Spiritual Life of Children*. Boston: Houghton Mifflin, 1990.
HOFFMAN, EDWARD. *Visions of Innocence: Spiritual and Inspirational Experiences of Childhood*. Boston: Shambhala Publications, 1992.
JOHNSON, LOUANNE. *School Is Not a Four-Letter Word*. New York: Hyperion, 1997.
MONTESSORI, MARIA. *The Absorbent Mind*. New York: Henry Holt, 1995.
———. *The Montessori Method*. New York: Schocken Books, 1988.
———. *Spontaneous Activity in Education*. Sage, Calif.: Education Systems, 1984.

HEALING AND DEALING WITH THE UNEXPECTED

DE PUY, CANDACE, AND DANA DOVITCH. *The Healing Choice: Your Guide to Emotional Recovery after an Abortion*. Simon and Schuster/Fireside, 1997.
ENGLISH, JANE BUTTERFIELD. *Different Doorway: Adventures of a Cesarean Born*. Point Reyes Station, Calif.: Earth Heart, 1985.
HARRISON, HELEN. *The Premature Baby Book: A Parent's Guide to Coping and Caring in the First Years*. New York: St. Martin's, 1984.
ILSE, SHEROKEE, AND LINDA BURNS. *Empty Arms: Coping after Miscarriage, Stillbirth and Infant Death*. Rev. ed. Minneapolis, Minn.: Wintergreen Press, 1990.
JASON, JANINE. *Parenting Your Premature Baby*. New York: Doubleday, 1990.
KÜBLER-ROSS, ELISABETH. *On Children and Death*. New York: Macmillan, 1993.

RESOURCE GUIDE

ON THE WEB

See also specific organizations listed in the next section for Web site addresses.

Family.com (www.family.com)
Disney's Webzine featuring authoritative parenting articles.

Health World Online (www.healthy.net)
Alternative and complementary health. Includes Lucia Capacchione's Creative Journal page: www.healthy.net/creativejournal

Lucia Capacchione's Web Site
www.luciac.com

Midlife Mommies (www.midlifemommies.com)
Internet magazine for women raising children in midlife (for dads, too).

ParentsPlace.com (www.parentsplace.com)
Bulletin boards, chat rooms, and professional columns on parenting and childrearing.

ORGANIZATIONS

ADOPTION

Adoptive Families of America
Offers support services for adoptive parents. Publications: *Adoptive*

Families magazine and a comprehensive catalogue of adoptive services throughout the United States.

> 2309 Como Ave., St. Paul, MN 55108
> Phone: (800) 372-3300
> Web site: www.adoptivefam.org

The Heritage Key

Provides educational information on other cultures and cross-cultural adoption.

> 6102 E. Mescal St., Scottsdale, AZ 85254-5419
> Phone: (602) 483-3313
> Web site: www.heritagekey.com

National Council for Adoption

> 1930 17th St. NW, Washington, DC 20009
> Phone: (202) 328-8072 (hot line) or (202) 328-1200
>   (information)
> E-mail: ncfa@juno.com

CHILDREN WITH SPECIAL NEEDS

Alliance of Genetic Support Groups

National coalition of support groups addressing the needs of individuals and families affected by genetic disorders.

> 4302 Connecticut Ave. NW, Suite 404, Washington, DC 20008
> Phone: (800) 336-4363
> E-mail: info@geneticalliance.org
> Web site: www.geneticalliance.org

American Cleft Palate Foundation

Information for parents of children with cleft palate, including feeding, dental care, and referrals to local professionals and support groups.

> 1829 E. Franklin St., Suite 1022, Chapel Hill, NC 27514
> Phone: (800) 24-CLEFT
> E-mail: cleftline@aol.com
> Web site: www.cleft.com

National Down's Syndrome Congress

Information service and hot line.

> 1605 Chantilly Dr., Suite 250, Atlanta, GA 30324
> Phone: (808) 232-6372
> E-mail: ndsccenter@aol.com
> Web site: www.members.carol.net/ndsc/

FAMILY SERVICES

Grief Recovery Helpline
Telephone support for those facing any significant loss.
> Phone: (800) 445-4808

Salvation Army Family Service
Provides a variety of services to parents and children.
> See the "Salvation Army" listing in your local phone book.

Self-Esteem Center
Offers information and guidance in parenting and family matters.
> 16535 9th Ave. N, Plymouth, MN 55447
> Phone: (612) 473-1840

HEALTH

American Holistic Medical Association
Organization of medical professionals (and students) practicing holistic medicine. Publication: *Holistic Medicine Quarterly.*

American Holistic Nurses Association
Organization of professional nurses practicing holistic medicine. Publication: *Journal of Holistic Nursing.*
> P.O. Box 2130, Flagstaff, AZ 86003-2130
> Phone: (800) 278-2462, (703) 556-9728, or (703) 556-9245

Boston Women's Health Book Collective
Grassroots women's health organization, creators of the pioneering and comprehensive health guide for women *Our Bodies, Ourselves.*
> 240A Elm St., Davis Square, Somerville, MA 02144
> Phone: (617) 625-0271
> E-mail: bwhc@iqc.apc.org

National Women's Health Network
Consumer-advocacy group providing information on women's health issues. Publication: *Network News* (for members only).
> 514 10th St. NW, Suite 400, Washington, DC 20004
> Phone: (202) 628-7814 (information clearinghouse line)

PREGNANCY AND CHILDBIRTH

American College of Nurse Midwives (ACNM)
Official professional organization for nurse-midwives in the United States. Publication: *Journal of Nurse-Midwifery* (for members only).

818 Connecticut Ave., Suite 900, Washington, DC 20006
Phone: (202) 728-9860
Fax: (202) 728-9879
E-mail: info@acnm.org
Web site: www.midwife.org

American College of Obstetricians and Gynecologists (ACOG)
The official organization for gynecologists and obstetricians in the United States.

409 12th St. SW, Washington, DC 20024
Phone: (202) 638-5577
Web site: www.acog.org

ASPO/Lamaze (American Society for Psychoprophylaxis Obstetrics)
Official organization for the Lamaze method of natural childbirth. Publications: *Lamaze Parents' Magazine* and *Journal of Perinatal Education*.

1200 19th St. NW, Suite 300, Washington, DC 20036
Phone: (800) 368-4404
Web site: lamaze-childbirth.com

Association for Care of Children's Health
Organization dedicated to improving intensive-care experiences for babies, parents, and caregivers.

19 Mantua Rd., Mt. Royal, NJ 08061
Phone: (800) 88-ACCH or (609) 224-1742

Association for Childhood Education International (ACEI)
17904 Georgia Ave., Suite 215, Olney, MD 20832
Phone: (301) 570-2111
Fax: (301) 570-2212
E-mail: aceihq@aol.com

Birth and Life Bookstore
Complete source of books, videotapes, and audiotapes about pregnancy, childbirth, newborns, and family life. Mail order available.

141 Commercial St. NE, Salem, OR 97301
Phone: (503) 371-4445
E-mail: onecascade@worldnet.att.net
Web site: 1cascade.com

Ask Dr. Gayle
Dr. Gayle Peterson answers questions from parents and spouses about marriage, family, and parenting topics. Includes training in prenatal and birth educational counseling.

1749 Vine St., Berkeley, CA 94703
Phone: (510) 526-5951
Web site: *www.askdrgayle.com*
(Dr. Peterson is the family therapist on *www.parentsplace.com*)

The Bradley Method
Information about training for mothers and coaches desiring natural childbirth.

P.O. Box 5224, Sherman Oaks, CA 91413-5224
Phone: (800) 423-2397 (outside of California) or (800) 42-BIRTH (in California)

Cesarean/Support, Education, and Concern (C/SEC)
Organization providing support and information on prevention of cesarean section delivery and recovery from cesareans.

22 Forest Rd., Framingham, MA 01701
Phone: (508) 877-8266

The Confinement Line
Referral service providing support for expectant mothers confined to bed during pregnancy.

P.O. Box 1609, Springfield, VA 22151
Phone: (703) 941-7183

Doulas of North America
Organization of childbirth assistants.

1100 23d Ave. E, Seattle, WA 98112
Phone: (206) 324-5440
Fax: (206) 325-0472
Web site: www.dona.com

Global Maternal/Child Health Association
Resource and referral service for water birth. Publication: *Water Birth Information Book.*

P.O. Box 1400, Wilsonville, OR 97070
Phone: (800) 641-BABY or (503) 682-3600
Fax: (503) 682-3434
E-mail: waterbirth@aol.com

International Association of Parents and Professionals for Safe Alternatives in Childbirth (NAPSAC)
Information and resource organization dedicated to freedom of choice in childbearing. Publication: *NAPSAC News* (for members only).

Route 4, Box 646, Marble Hill, MO 63764
Phone: (573) 238-2010

International Childbirth Education Association (ICEA)
Networking and resource organization for childbirth education. Publications: *International Journal of Childbirth Education* (for members only), *ICEA Publications Catalog.*
>P.O. Box 20048, Minneapolis, MN 55420-0048
>Phone: (612) 854-8660
>E-mail: info@icea.org
>Web site: www.icea.org

La Leche League International (LLLI)
Resource and information network on breast-feeding. Publications: *La Leche League International Catalog* and *La Leche League Brochure for Breast Feeding Reference Library Database.*
>1400 N. Meacham Rd., Schaumburg, IL 60173-4840
>Phone: (800) LA LECHE or (847) 519-7730
>Fax: (847) 519-0035
>Web site: www.lalecheleague.org

National Association of Childbearing Centers (NACC)
Referral center for birthing centers approved by the NACC.
>3123 Gottschall Rd., Perkiomenville, PA 18074
>Phone: (800) 868-NACA

Pregnancy and Infant Loss Center
A national nonprofit organization offering support, resources, and education on infant death.
>1421 E. Wayzata Blvd., Suite 30, Wayzata, MN 55391
>Phone: (612) 473-9372

Resolve
Pamphlets and information about infertility and pregnancy loss. When requesting information by mail, include a self-addressed, stamped envelope.
>1310 Broadway, Somerville, MA 02144-1731
>Phone: (617) 623-1156 (general information) or (617) 623-0744 (help line)

SHARE
Pregnancy and infant-loss support services. Publication: *Sharing,* newsletter for bereaved parents.
>Saint Joseph Health Center, National SHARE Office
>300 First Capitol Dr., St. Charles, MO 63301-2893
>Phone: (800) 821-6819 and (314) 947-6164
>Web site: *www.nationalshareoffice.com*

Sidelines National Support Network

Nonprofit organization dedicated to providing support and information about high-risk pregnancies. Its experienced volunteers have had high-risk pregnancies themselves. Services include telephone peer counseling and community referrals. Publications: *Leftside Lines* magazine, and educational literature.

P.O. Pox 1808, Laguna Beach, CA 92652

Phone: (949) 497-2265

Web site: *www.sidelines.org*

Sudden Infant Death Syndrome (SIDS) Alliance

Nonprofit health organization of volunteers dedicated to supporting SIDS families and SIDS research.

1314 Bedford Ave., Suite 210, Baltimore, MD 21208

Phone: (800) 221-SIDS (24-hour toll-free hot line—information and referrals) or (530) 553-7702

Fax: (530) 533-798